Curvy CROCHET

CROCHETED FASHIONS THAT FLATTER YOUR FIGURE? WITH *CURVY CROCHET*, THAT'S EXACTLY WHAT YOU GET! LIGHTWEIGHT YARN GIVES THESE FEMININE DESIGNS THE EASY-WEARING, BEAUTIFUL DRAPE THAT LOOKS SO GOOD ON YOUR CURVES. THE LACY PEASANT TOP IS SCRUMPTIOUS WITH ITS BREEZY DESIGN. FOR A CAREFREE STYLE YOU'LL WANT TO REACH FOR EVERY DAY, MAKE A TIEBACK TUNIC. THERE'S ALSO A RIBBED WAIST VEST THAT SKIMS YOUR BODY JUST RIGHT—NOT TOO SNUG, NOT TOO LOOSE. AND HOW ABOUT A MUST-HAVE ACCESSORY OR TWO, SUCH AS THE GLAMOUROUS BEADED STOLE OR THE FELTED HANDBAG? CREATE YOUR FAVORITE GARMENTS FROM THIS COLLECTION AND KNOW THAT YOU LOOK AMAZING IN CROCHET!

Talent—Times Two!

MARLAINA BIRD

JILL WRIGHT

Crocheters everywhere would have missed out on a good thing if Marlaina Bird of Yarn Thing podcast fame had never met her husband. That's because her hubby's step-mom just happens to be designer Jill Wright of Woolcrafting.com, an online site filled with articles about yarn crafts.

Together, the creative women make an amazing design team.

As Marlaina says, "Jill and I quickly became best friends, and we discovered we work well together. We're very different in how we approach our work. She's the collected, very organized type. I'm excitable and outgoing, and tend to procrastinate a little. If I'm stuck on a design element and a deadline is approaching, Jill's calm outlook inspires me to work through it."

Jill adds, "When we take on a project together, we both work on drafting patterns and deciding on swatches and yarns. When it comes to designing, Marlaina is confident about a new idea right away. I'm methodical and like more time to work out the concept. We complement each other."

Marlaina's blogtalkradio.com podcasts include interviews of personalities in the knit and crochet industry. She also blogs on ThePurseWorkshop.com.

Jill's background includes studies in clothing design and textile management.

Both Jill and Marlaina are proud moms, each having three children who help keep things lively.

LEISURE ARTS, INC.
Little Rock, Arkansas

Cowl Neck Tunic

◗◼◻◻ **EASY**

Size	Finished Chest Measurement
Large	42^1/$_2$" (108 cm)
Extra Large	46" (117 cm)
2X-Large	50^1/$_2$" (128.5 cm)
3X-Large	54" (137 cm)
4X-Large	58^1/$_2$" (148.5 cm)

Size Note: Instructions are written with sizes Large and Extra Large in the first set of braces { } and with sizes 2X-Large, 3X-Large, and 4X-Large in the second set of braces. Instructions will be easier to read if you circle all the numbers pertaining to your size. If only one number is given, it applies to all sizes.

MATERIALS

LIGHT 3

Light Weight Yarn
[3 ounces, 251 yards
(85 grams, 230 meters) per skein]:
    {10-12}{15-16-18} skeins
Crochet hooks, sizes E (3.5 mm) **and**
    F (3.75 mm) **or** sizes needed for gauge
Tapestry needle

GAUGE: With smaller size hook, in pattern,
    [dc, (ch 2, dc) twice] 5 times
    and 16 rows = 4" (10 cm)

Gauge Swatch: 4^1/$_2$" x 4" (11.5 cm x 10 cm)
With smaller size hook, ch 29.
Work same as Body for 16 rows.
Finish off.

STITCH GUIDE

DECREASE (uses next 2 sts or sps)
★ YO, insert hook in **next** st or sp, YO and pull up a loop, YO and draw through 2 loops on hook; repeat from ★ once **more**, YO and draw through all 3 loops on hook (**counts as one dc**).

Back

With smaller size hook, ch {134-144}{159-169-184}.

Row 1 (Right side)**:** Dc in sixth ch from hook **(first 3 skipped chs count as first dc, now and throughout)**, (ch 2, dc in same ch) twice, ★ skip next 4 chs, dc in next ch, (ch 2, dc in same ch) twice; repeat from ★ across to last 3 chs, skip next 2 chs, dc in last ch: {52-56}{62-66-72} ch-2 sps.

Note: Loop a short piece of yarn around any stitch to mark Row 1 as **right** side.

Row 2: Ch 4 **(counts as first hdc plus ch 2)**, turn; sc in next ch-2 sp, ch 3, sc in next ch-2 sp, ★ ch 4, sc in next ch-2 sp, ch 3, sc in next ch-2 sp; repeat from ★ across, ch 2, skip next dc, hdc in last dc: {53-57}{63-67-73} sps.

Row 3: Ch 3 **(counts as first dc, now and throughout)**, turn; skip next ch-2 sp, dc in next ch-3 sp, (ch 2, dc in same sp) twice, ★ skip next ch-4 sp, dc in next ch-3 sp, (ch 2, dc in same sp) twice; repeat from ★ across to last ch-2 sp, skip last ch-2 sp, dc in last hdc: {52-56}{62-66-72} ch-2 sps.

Rows 4-16: Repeat Rows 2 and 3, 6 times; then repeat Row 2 once **more**: {53-57}{63-67-73} sps.

WAIST SHAPING

Row 1: Ch 2 (**counts as first hdc, now and throughout**), turn; skip next ch-2 sp, (2 dc, ch 2, dc) in next ch-3 sp, ★ skip next ch-4 sp, dc in next ch-3 sp, (ch 2, dc in same sp) twice; repeat from ★ across to last 3 sps, skip next ch-4 sp, (dc, ch 2, 2 dc) in next ch-3 sp, skip last ch-2 sp, hdc in last hdc: {50-54} {60-64-70} ch-2 sps.

Row 2: Ch 2, turn; skip next dc, sc in sp **before** next dc *(Fig. 5, page 59)*, ch 3, ★ sc in next ch-2 sp, ch 4, sc in next ch-2 sp, ch 3; repeat from ★ across to last 3 sts, skip next dc, sc in sp **before** next dc, skip next dc, hdc in last hdc: {51-55}{61-65-71} sps.

Row 3: Ch 3, turn; (dc, ch 2, dc) in next ch-3 sp, ★ skip next ch-4 sp, dc in next ch-3 sp, (ch 2, dc in same sp) twice; repeat from ★ across to last 2 sps, skip next ch-4 sp, (dc, ch 2, dc) in last ch-3 sp, dc in last hdc: {50-54}{60-64-70} ch-2 sps.

Row 4: Ch 4 (**counts as first dc plus ch 1**), turn; sc in next ch-2 sp, ch 4, sc in next ch-2 sp, ★ ch 3, sc in next ch-2 sp, ch 4, sc in next ch-2 sp; repeat from ★ across, ch 1, skip next dc, dc in last dc: {51-55}{61-65-71} sps.

Instructions continued on page 4.

Row 5: Ch 5 (counts as first dc plus ch 2, now and throughout), turn; dc in next ch-1 sp, ★ skip next ch-4 sp, dc in next ch-3 sp, (ch 2, dc in same sp) twice; repeat from ★ across to last 2 sps, skip next ch-4 sp, dc in next ch-1 sp, ch 2, dc in last dc: {50-54}{60-64-70} ch-2 sps.

Row 6: Ch 1, turn; sc in next ch-2 sp, ch 4, sc in next ch-2 sp, ★ ch 3, sc in next ch-2 sp, ch 4, sc in next ch-2 sp; repeat from ★ across to last dc, leave last dc unworked: {49-53}{59-63-69} sps.

Row 7: Ch 3, turn; ★ skip next ch-4 sp, dc in next ch-3 sp, (ch 2, dc in same sp) twice; repeat from ★ across to last ch-4 sp, skip last ch-4 sp, dc in last sc: {48-52}{58-62-68} ch-2 sps.

Row 8: Ch 4 (counts as first hdc plus ch 2), turn; sc in next ch-2 sp, ch 3, sc in next ch-2 sp, ★ ch 4, sc in next ch-2 sp, ch 3, sc in next ch-2 sp; repeat from ★ across, ch 2, skip next dc, hdc in last dc: {49-53}{59-63-69} sps.

Row 9: Ch 5, turn; skip next ch-2 sp, (dc, ch 2, dc) in next ch-3 sp, ★ skip next ch-4 sp, dc in next ch-3 sp, (ch 2, dc in same sp) twice; repeat from ★ across to last 3 sps, skip next ch-4 sp, (dc, ch 2, dc) in next ch-3 sp, ch 2, skip next ch-2 sp, dc in last hdc: {48-52}{58-62-68} ch-2 sps.

Row 10: Ch 1, turn; sc in next ch-2 sp, ch 3, sc in next ch-2 sp, ★ ch 4, sc in next ch-2 sp, ch 3, sc in next ch-2 sp; repeat from ★ across, leave last dc unworked: {47-51}{57-61-67} sps.

Row 11: Ch 5, turn; (dc, ch 2, dc) in next ch-3 sp, ★ skip next ch-4 sp, dc in next ch-3 sp, (ch 2, dc in same sp) twice; repeat from ★ across to last 2 sps, skip next ch-4 sp, (dc, ch 2, dc) in last ch-3 sp, ch 2, dc in last sc: {48-52}{58-62-68} ch-2 sps.

Rows 12-22: Repeat Rows 10 and 11, 5 times; then repeat Row 10 once **more**: {47-51}{57-61-67} sps.

BODY SHAPING

Row 1: Ch 2, turn; (2 dc, ch 2, dc) in next ch-3 sp, ★ skip next ch-4 sp, dc in next ch-3 sp, (ch 2, dc in same sp) twice; repeat from ★ across to last 2 sps, skip next ch-4 sp, (dc, ch 2, 2 dc) in last ch-3 sp, hdc in last sc: {46-50}{56-60-66} ch-2 sps.

Row 2: Ch 4 (counts as first hdc plus ch 2), turn; skip next dc, sc in sp **before** next dc, ★ ch 3, sc in next ch-2 sp, ch 4, sc in next ch-2 sp; repeat from ★ across, ch 3, skip next dc, sc in sp **before** next dc, ch 2, skip next dc, hdc in last dc: {49-53}{59-63-69} sps.

Row 3: Ch 3, turn; dc in next ch-2 sp, (ch 2, dc in same sp) twice, dc in next ch-3 sp, (ch 2, dc in same sp) twice, ★ skip next ch-4 sp, dc in next ch-3 sp, (ch 2, dc in same sp) twice; repeat from ★ across to last ch-2 sp, dc in last ch-2 sp, (ch 2, dc in same sp) twice, dc in last hdc: {52-56}{62-66-72} ch-2 sps.

Row 4: Ch 4 (counts as first hdc plus ch 2), turn; sc in next ch-2 sp, ch 3, sc in next ch-2 sp, ★ ch 4, sc in next ch-2 sp, ch 3, sc in next ch-2 sp; repeat from ★ across, ch 2, skip next dc, hdc in last dc: {53-57}{63-67-73} sps.

Row 5: Ch 3, turn; skip next ch-2 sp, dc in next ch-3 sp, (ch 2, dc in same sp) twice, ★ skip next ch-4 sp, dc in next ch-3 sp, (ch 2, dc in same sp) twice; repeat from ★ across to last ch-2 sp, skip last ch-2 sp, dc in last hdc: {52-56}{62-66-72} ch-2 sps.

Rows 6-26: Repeat Rows 4 and 5, 10 times; then repeat Row 4 once **more**: {53-57}{63-67-73} sps.

Finish off.

ARMHOLE SHAPING

Row 1: With **right** side facing and using smaller size hook, skip first 3 sps and join yarn with dc in next ch-3 sp *(see Joining With Dc, page 58)*; dc in next sc, ★ skip next ch-4 sp, dc in next ch-3 sp, (ch 2, dc in same sp) twice; repeat from ★ across to last 5 sps, skip next ch-4 sp, dc in next sc and in next ch-3 sp, leave remaining sts unworked: {44-48}{54-58-64} ch-2 sps.

Row 2: Ch 3, turn; sc in next ch-2 sp, ch 3, sc in next ch-2 sp, ★ ch 4, sc in next ch-2 sp, ch 3, sc in next ch-2 sp; repeat from ★ across, skip next 2 dc, dc in last dc: {43-47}{53-57-63} sps.

Row 3: Turn; slip st in first 2 sts and in next ch-3 sp, ch 3, ★ skip next ch-4 sp, dc in next ch-3 sp, (ch 2, dc in same sp) twice; repeat from ★ across to last 2 sps, skip next ch-4 sp, dc in last ch-3 sp, leave remaining sts unworked: {40-44}{50-54-60} ch-2 sps.

Row 4 (Decrease row): Turn, slip st in first 2 dc, ch 1, sc in next ch-2 sp, ch 3, sc in next ch-2 sp, ★ ch 4, sc in next ch-2 sp, ch 3, sc in next ch-2 sp; repeat from ★ across, leave last 2 dc unworked: {39-43}{49-53-59} sps.

Row 5 (Decrease row): Turn; slip st in first sc and in next ch-3 sp, ch 5, dc in same sp, ★ skip next ch-4 sp, dc in next ch-3 sp, (ch 2, dc in same sp) twice; repeat from ★ across to last 2 sps, skip next ch-4 sp, (dc, ch 2, dc) in last ch-2 sp: {38-42}{48-52-58} ch-2 sps.

Row 6 (Decrease row): Ch 1, turn; sc in next ch-2 sp, ch 4, sc in next ch-2 sp, ★ ch 3, sc in next ch-2 sp, ch 4, sc in next ch-2 sp; repeat from ★ across, leave last dc unworked: {37-41}{47-51-57} sps.

Row 7 (Decrease row): Ch 3, turn; dc in next 2 sps, (ch 2, dc in same sp) twice, ★ skip next ch-4 sp, dc in next ch-3 sp, (ch 2, dc in same sp) twice; repeat from ★ across to last ch-4 sp, dc in last ch-4 sp and in last sc: {36-40} {46-50-56} ch-2 sps.

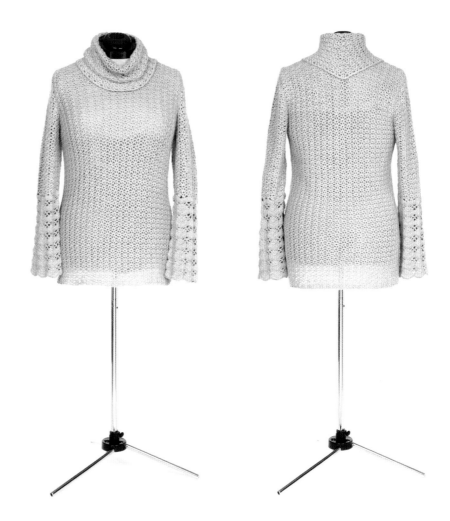

Sizes 2X-Large, 3X-Large, and 4X-Large Only
Row 8: Turn; slip st in first 3 dc, ch 1, sc in next ch-2 sp, ch 3, sc in next ch-2 sp, ★ ch 4, sc in next ch-2 sp, ch 3, sc in next ch-2 sp; repeat from ★ across, leave last 3 dc unworked: {45-49-55} sps.

Sizes 2X-Large and 3X-Large Only
Rows 9-11: Repeat Rows 5-7 once: {42-46} ch-2 sps.

Size 4X-Large Only
Rows 9-15: Repeat Rows 5-8 once, then repeat Rows 5-7 once **more**: 48 ch-2 sps.

All Sizes
Next Row: Turn; skip first dc, slip st in sp **before** next dc, ch 1, sc in same sp, ch 4, ★ sc in next ch-2 sp, ch 3, sc in next ch-2 sp, ch 4; repeat from ★ across, skip next 2 dc, sc in sp **before** last dc, leave last dc unworked: {37-41}{43-47-49} sps.

Instructions continued on page 6.

Next Row: Ch 3, turn; dc in next 2 sps, (ch 2, dc in same sp) twice, ★ skip next ch-4 sp, dc in next ch-3 sp, (ch 2, dc in same sp) twice; repeat from ★ across to last ch-4 sp, dc in last ch-4 sp and in last sc: {36-40}{42-46-48} ch-2 sps.

Repeat last 2 rows for pattern until Armholes measure approximately {7³/₄-8¹/₄}{9¹/₂-10¹/₂-11}"/{19.5-21}{24-26.5-28} cm, ending by working a **right** side row.

Finish off.

Front

Work same as Back through Row {6-6}{8-10-14} of Armhole Shaping: {37-41}{45-47-49} sps.

LEFT NECK SHAPING

Row 1: Ch 3, turn; dc in first 2 sps, (ch 2, dc in same sp) twice, skip next ch-4 sp, dc in next ch-3 sp, ★ (ch 2, dc in same sp) twice, skip next ch-4 sp, dc in next ch-3 sp; repeat from ★ {5-6}{6-7-8} times **more**; leave remaining sts unworked: {14-16}{16-18-20} ch-2 sps.

Row 2: Turn; slip st in first 2 dc, ch 1, sc in next ch-2 sp, ch 3, sc in next ch-2 sp, ★ ch 4, sc in next ch-2 sp, ch 3, sc in next ch-2 sp; repeat from ★ across, ch 4, skip next 2 dc, sc in sp **before** last dc, leave last dc unworked.

Row 3: Ch 3, turn; ★ skip next ch-4 sp, dc in next ch-3 sp, (ch 2, dc in same sp) twice; repeat from ★ across to last 2 sps, skip next ch-4 sp, (dc, ch 2, dc) in last ch-3 sp, leave remaining sts unworked: {13-15}{15-17-19} ch-2 sps.

Row 4: Ch 1, turn; skip first dc, sc in next ch-2 sp, ★ ch 4, sc in next ch-2 sp, ch 3, sc in next ch-2 sp; repeat from ★ across, ch 4, skip next dc, sc in sp **before** last dc, leave last dc unworked.

Row 5: Ch 3, turn; ★ skip next ch-4 sp, dc in next ch-3 sp, (ch 2, dc in same sp) twice; repeat from ★ across to last ch-4 sp, skip last ch-4 sp, dc in last sc: {12-14}{14-16-18} ch-2 sps.

Row 6: Ch 1, turn; slip st in first 2 dc, sc in next ch-2 sp, ch 3, sc in next ch-2 sp, ★ ch 4, sc in next ch-2 sp, ch 3, sc in next ch-2 sp; repeat from ★ across, ch 4, skip next dc, sc in sp **before** last dc, leave last dc unworked.

Row 7: Ch 3, turn; ★ skip next ch-4 sp, dc in next ch-3 sp, (ch 2, dc in same sp) twice; repeat from ★ across to last 2 sps, skip next ch-4 sp, (dc, ch 2, dc) in last ch-3 sp: {11-13}{13-15-17} ch-2 sps.

Row 8: Repeat Row 4.

Size 4X-Large Only

Row 9: Ch 3, turn; ★ skip next ch-4 sp, dc in next ch-3 sp, (ch 2, dc in same sp) twice; repeat from ★ across to last 3 sps, skip next ch-4 sp, (dc, ch 2, dc) in next ch-3 sp, skip last ch-4 sp, dc in last sc: 15 ch-2 sps.

Row 10: Repeat Row 2.

Row 11: Repeat Row 5: 14 ch-2 sps.

Row 12: Ch 1, turn; skip first dc, sc in sp **before** next dc, ★ ch 4, sc in next ch-2 sp, ch 3, sc in next ch-2 sp; repeat from ★ across, ch 4, skip next dc, sc in sp **before** last dc, leave last dc unworked: 15 sps.

All Sizes

Next Row: Ch 3, turn; ★ skip next ch-4 sp, dc in next ch-3 sp, (ch 2, dc in same sp) twice; repeat from ★ across to last ch-4 sp, dc in last ch-4 sp and in last sc: {10-12}{12-14-14} ch-2 sps.

Next Row: Ch 1, turn; skip first dc, sc in sp **before** next dc, ★ ch 4, sc in next ch-2 sp, ch 3, sc in next ch-2 sp; repeat from ★ across, ch 4, skip next dc, sc in sp **before** last dc, leave last dc unworked: {11-13}{13-15-15} sps.

Repeat last 2 rows for pattern until Armhole measures same as Back, ending by working a **right** side row; finish off.

RIGHT NECK SHAPING

Row 1: With **right** side facing and using smaller size hook, skip next {5-5}{5-7-5} sps from Left Neck Shaping and join yarn with dc in next ch-3 sp; ★ skip next ch-4 sp, dc in next ch-3 sp, (ch 2, dc in same sp) twice; repeat from ★ across to last ch-4 sp, dc in last ch-4 sp and in last sc: {14-16}{16-18-20} ch-2 sps.

Row 2: Ch 1, turn; skip first dc, sc in sp **before** next dc, ★ ch 4, sc in next ch-2 sp, ch 3, sc in next ch-2 sp; repeat from ★ across, leave last 2 dc unworked.

Row 3 (Decrease row): Ch 5, turn; dc in next ch-3 sp, ★ skip next ch-4 sp, dc in next ch-3 sp, (ch 2, dc in same sp) twice; repeat from ★ across to last ch-4 sp, skip last ch-4 sp, dc in last sc: {13-15}{17-17-19} ch-2 sps.

Row 4: Ch 1, turn; skip first dc, sc in sp **before** next dc, ch 4, sc in next ch-2 sp, ★ ch 3, sc in next ch-2 sp, ch 4, sc in next ch-2 sp; repeat from ★ across, leave last dc unworked.

Row 5 (Decrease row): Ch 3, turn; ★ skip next ch-4 sp, dc in next ch-3 sp, (ch 2, dc in same sp) twice; repeat from ★ across to last ch-4 sp, skip last ch-4 sp, dc in last sc: {12-14}{16-16-18} ch-2 sps.

Rows 6-8: Repeat Rows 2-4: {11-13}{15-15-17} sps.

Size 4X-Large Only
Row 9: Ch 3, turn; skip next ch-4 sp, (dc, ch 2, dc) in next ch-3 sp, ★ skip next ch-4 sp, dc in next ch-3 sp, (ch 2, dc in same sp) twice; repeat from ★ across to last ch-4 sp, skip last ch-4 sp, dc in last sc: 15 ch-2 sps.

Instructions continued on page 8.

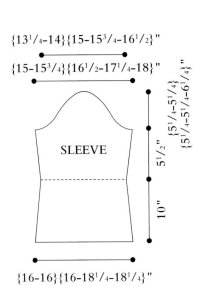

{13^1/$_4$-14}{15-15^3/$_4$-16^1/$_2$}"

{15-15^3/$_4$}{16^1/$_2$-17^1/$_4$-18}"

SLEEVE

5^1/$_2$" {5^1/$_4$-5^1/$_4$}{5^1/$_4$-5^1/$_4$-6^1/$_4$}"

10"

{16-16}{16-18^1/$_4$-18^1/$_4$}"

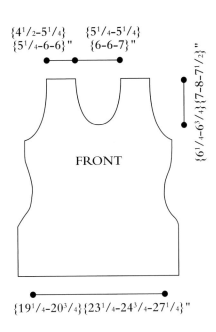

{4^1/$_2$-5^1/$_4$} {5^1/$_4$-5^1/$_4$}
{5^1/$_4$-6-6} {6-6-7}"

FRONT

{6^1/$_4$-6^3/$_4$}{7-8-7^1/$_2$}"

{19^1/$_4$-20^3/$_4$}{23^1/$_4$-24^3/$_4$-27^1/$_4$}"

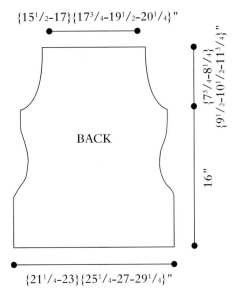

{15^1/$_2$-17}{17^3/$_4$-19^1/$_2$-20^1/$_4$}"

BACK

{7^3/$_4$-8^1/$_4$}{9^1/$_2$-10^1/$_2$-11^3/$_4$}"

16"

{21^1/$_4$-23}{25^1/$_4$-27-29^1/$_4$}"

All Sizes

Next Row: Ch 3, turn; ★ skip next ch-4 sp, dc in next ch-3 sp, (ch 2, dc in same sp) twice; repeat from ★ across to last ch-4 sp, skip last ch-4 sp, dc in last sc: {10-12}{14-14-14} ch-2 sps.

Next Row: Ch 1, turn; skip first dc, sc in sp **before** next dc, ★ ch 4, sc in next ch-2 sp, ch 3, sc in next ch-2 sp; repeat from ★ across, ch 4, skip next dc, sc in sp **before** last dc, leave last dc unworked: {11-13}{15-15-15} sps.

Repeat last 2 rows for pattern until Armhole measures same as Back, ending by working a **right** side row.

Finish off.

Sleeve (Make 2)

With smaller size hook, ch {84-89}{94-99-104}.

Row 1 (Right side)**:** Dc in sixth ch from hook, (ch 2, dc in same ch) twice, ★ skip next 4 chs, dc in next ch, (ch 2, dc in same ch) twice; repeat from ★ across to last 3 chs, skip next 2 chs, dc in last ch: {32-34} {36-38-40} ch-2 sps.

Note: Mark Row 1 as **right** side.

Row 2: Ch 4 (counts as first hdc plus ch 2), turn; sc in next ch-2 sp, ch 3, sc in next ch-2 sp, ★ ch 4, sc in next ch-2 sp, ch 3, sc in next ch-2 sp; repeat from ★ across, ch 2, skip next dc, hdc in last dc: {33-35}{37-39-41} sps.

Row 3: Ch 3, turn; dc in same st, skip next ch-2 sp, dc in next ch-3 sp, (ch 2, dc in same sp) twice, ★ skip next ch-4 sp, dc in next ch-3 sp, (ch 2, dc in same sp) twice; repeat from ★ across to last ch-2 sp, skip last ch-2 sp, 2 dc in last hdc: {32-34}{36-38-40} ch-2 sps.

Row 10: Ch 1, turn; skip first dc, sc in sp **before** next dc, ch 4, sc in next ch-2 sp, ★ ch 3, sc in next ch-2 sp, ch 4, sc in next ch-2 sp; repeat from ★ across.

Row 11: Repeat Row 5: 14 ch-2 sps.

Row 12: Ch 1, turn; skip first dc, sc in sp **before** next dc, ★ ch 4, sc in next ch-2 sp, ch 3, sc in next ch-2 sp; repeat from ★ across, ch 4, skip next dc, sc in sp **before** last dc, leave last dc unworked: 15 sps.

Row 4: Ch 4 (**counts as first dc plus ch 1**), turn; skip first dc, sc in sp **before** next dc, ★ ch 4, sc in next ch-2 sp, ch 3, sc in next ch-2 sp; repeat from ★ across, ch 4, skip next 2 dc, sc in sp **before** last dc, ch 1, dc in last dc: {35-37}{39-41-43} sps.

Row 5: Ch 3, turn; dc in same st, skip next 2 sps, dc in next ch-3 sp, (ch 2, dc in same sp) twice, ★ skip next ch-4 sp, dc in next ch-3 sp, (ch 2, dc in same sp) twice; repeat from ★ across to last 2 sps, skip last 2 sps, 2 dc in last dc: {32-34}{36-38-40} ch-2 sps.

Row 6: Repeat Row 4: {35-37}{39-41-43} sps.

Row 7: Ch 5, turn; dc in next ch-1 sp, ★ skip next ch-4 sp, dc in next ch-3 sp, (ch 2, dc in same sp) twice; repeat from ★ across to last 2 sps, skip next ch-4 sp, dc in last ch-1 sp, ch 2, dc in last dc: {34-36}{38-40-42} ch-2 sps.

Row 8: Ch 1, turn; (sc, ch 3, sc) in next ch-2 sp, ch 4, ★ sc in next ch-2 sp, ch 3, sc in next ch-2 sp, ch 4; repeat from ★ across to last ch-2 sp, (sc, ch 3, sc) in last ch-2 sp, leave last dc unworked: {35-37}{39-41-43} sps.

Row 9: Ch 3, turn; dc in next ch-3 sp, (ch 2, dc in same sp) twice, ★ skip next ch-4 sp, dc in next ch-3 sp, (ch 2, dc in same sp) twice; repeat from ★ across, dc in last sc: {36-38}{40-42-44} ch-2 sps.

Row 10: Ch 1, turn; skip first dc, sc in sp **before** next dc, ★ ch 4, sc in next ch-2 sp, ch 3, sc in next ch-2 sp; repeat from ★ across, ch 4, skip next dc, sc in sp **before** last dc, leave last dc unworked: {37-39}{41-43-45} sps.

Row 11: Ch 3, turn; skip next ch-4 sp, dc in next ch-3 sp, (ch 2, dc in same sp) twice, ★ skip next ch-4 sp, dc in next ch-3 sp, (ch 2, dc in same sp) twice; repeat from ★ across to last ch-4 sp, skip last ch-4 sp, dc in last sc: {36-38}{40-42-44} ch-2 sps.

Rows 12-22: Repeat Rows 10 and 11, 5 times; then repeat Row 10 once **more**: {37-39}{41-43-45} sps.

Finish off.

CAP SHAPING

Row 1: With **right** side facing and using smaller size hook, skip first 3 sps and join yarn with dc in next ch-3 sp; dc in next sc, ★ skip next ch-4 sp, dc in next ch-3 sp, (ch 2, dc in same sp) twice; repeat from ★ across to last 5 sps, skip next ch-4 sp, dc in next sc and in next ch-3 sp, leave remaining sts unworked: {28-30}{32-34-36} ch-2 sps.

Row 2: Ch 3, turn; skip next 2 dc, sc in next ch-2 sp, ch 3, sc in next ch-2 sp, ★ ch 4, sc in next ch-2 sp, ch 3, sc in next ch-2 sp; repeat from ★ across to last 3 dc, skip next 2 dc, dc in last dc: {27-29}{31-33-35} sps.

Row 3: Turn; slip st in next ch-3 sp, ch 5, dc in same ch-3 sp, ★ skip next ch-4 sp, dc in next ch-3 sp, (ch 2, dc in same sp) twice; repeat from ★ across to last 2 sps, skip next ch-4 sp, (dc, ch 2, dc) in last ch-3 sp, leave last 2 sts unworked: {26-28}{30-32-34} ch-2 sps.

Row 4: Ch 1, turn; skip first dc, sc in next 2 ch-2 sps, ★ ch 3, sc in next ch-2 sp, ch 4, sc in next ch-2 sp; repeat from ★ across to last 2 ch-2 sps, ch 3, sc in last 2 ch-2 sps, leave last dc unworked: {23-25}{27-29-31} sps.

Row 5: Ch 3, turn; dc in next ch-3 sp, (ch 2, dc in same sp) twice, ★ skip next ch-4 sp, dc in next ch-3 sp, (ch 2, dc in same sp) twice; repeat from ★ across to last 2 sc, skip next sc, dc in last sc: {24-26}{28-30-32} ch-2 sps.

Row 6 (Decrease row)**:** Turn; slip st in first 2 dc, ch 1, sc in next ch-2 sp, ch 3, sc in next ch-2 sp, ★ ch 4, sc in next ch-2 sp, ch 3, sc in next ch-2 sp; repeat from ★ across, leave last 2 dc unworked: {23-25}{27-29-31} sps.

Instructions continued on page 10.

Row 7 (Decrease row): Ch 5, turn; dc in next ch-3 sp, ★ skip next ch-4 sp, dc in next ch-3 sp, (ch 2, dc in same sp) twice; repeat from ★ across to last 2 sps, skip next ch-4 sp, (dc, ch 2, dc) in last ch-3 sp: {22-24}{26-28-30} ch-2 sps.

Row 8 (Decrease row): Ch 1, turn; sc in next ch-2 sp, ch 4, sc in next ch-2 sp, ★ ch 3, sc in next ch-2 sp, ch 4, sc in next ch-2 sp; repeat from ★ across, leave last dc unworked: {21-23}{25-27-29} sps.

Row 9 (Decrease row): Ch 3, turn; ★ skip next ch-4 sp, dc in next ch-3 sp, (ch 2, dc in same sp) twice; repeat from ★ across to last ch-4 sp, skip last ch-4 sp, dc in last sc: {20-22}{24-26-28} ch-2 sps.

Rows 10 thru {19-19}{23-21-21}: Repeat Rows 6-9, {2-2}{3-3-3} times; then repeat Rows 6 and 7, {1-1}{1-0-0} time(s) **more (see Zeros, page 58):** {10-12}{10-14-16} ch-2 sps.

Finish off.

LOWER SLEEVE

Row 1: With **wrong** side facing and using larger size hook, join yarn with sc *(see Joining With Sc, page 58)* in first free loop on beginning ch *(Fig. 3b, page 59)*; work {91-91}{91-104-104} sc evenly spaced across: {92-92}{92-105-105} sc.

Row 2: Ch 3, turn; dc in next 3 sc, decrease 3 times, dc in next 3 sc, ★ 3 dc in next sc, dc in next 3 sc, decrease 3 times, dc in next 3 sc; repeat from ★ across to last sc, 2 dc in last sc. {84-84}{84-96-96} dc.

Row 3: Ch 3, turn; 2 dc in same st, ch 2, skip next 3 dc, sc in next dc, ch 4, skip next 3 dc, sc in next dc, ch 2, ★ skip next 3 dc, 5 dc in next dc, ch 2, skip next 3 dc, sc in next dc, ch 4, skip next 3 dc, sc in next dc, ch 2; repeat from ★ across to last 3 dc, skip next 2 dc, 3 dc in last dc.

Row 4: Ch 3, turn; dc in same st, 2 dc in next dc, dc in next dc, ch 2, skip next ch-2 sp, sc in next ch-4 sp, ch 2, skip next ch-2 sp, dc in next dc, ★ 2 dc in next dc, 3 dc in next dc, 2 dc in next dc, dc in next dc, ch 2, skip next ch-2 sp, sc in next ch-4 sp, ch 2, skip next ch-2 sp, dc in next dc; repeat from ★ across to last 2 dc, 2 dc in each of last 2 dc.

Row 5: Ch 3, turn; (2 dc in next dc, dc in next dc) twice, skip next 2 ch-2 sps, dc in next dc, ★ (2 dc in next dc, dc in next dc) 4 times, skip next 2 ch-2 sps, dc in next dc; repeat from ★ across to last 4 dc, (2 dc in next dc, dc in next dc) twice.

Row 6: Ch 3, turn; dc in next 3 dc, decrease 3 times, dc in next 3 dc, ★ 3 dc in next dc, dc in next 3 dc, decrease 3 times, dc in next 3 dc; repeat from ★ across to last dc, 2 dc in last dc.

Rows 7-30: Repeat Rows 3-6, 6 times.

Finish off.

Sew shoulder seams.

COWL

Rnd 1: With **wrong** side facing and using smaller size hook, join yarn with sc at center Back neck; work {15-15}{17-17-20} sc evenly spaced across Back neck, work 45 sc evenly spaced across left Neck edge, work {15-15}{21-21-25} sc evenly spaced across Front neck edge, work 45 sc evenly spaced across right Neck edge, work {15-15}{17-17-20} sc evenly spaced across Back neck; join with slip st to first sc: {136-136}{146-146-156} sc.

Rnd 2: Ch 3, do not turn; skip next 2 sc, dc in next sc, (ch 2, dc in same st) twice, ★ skip next 4 sc, dc in next sc, (ch 2, dc in same st) twice; repeat from ★ around to last 2 sc, skip last 2 sc; join with slip st to first dc: {54-54}{58-58-62} ch-2 sps.

Rnd 3: Ch 5, turn; sc in next ch-2 sp, ch 3, sc in next ch-2 sp, ★ ch 4, sc in next ch-2 sp, ch 3, sc in next ch-2 sp; repeat from ★ around, ch 2; join with slip st to first dc: {55-55}{59-59-63} sps.

Rnd 4: Ch 3, turn; skip next ch-2 sp, dc in next ch-3 sp, (ch 2, dc in same sp) twice, ★ skip next ch-4 sp, dc in next ch-3 sp, (ch 2, dc in same sp) twice; repeat from ★ around to last ch-2 sp, skip last ch-2 sp; join with slip st to first dc: {54-54}{58-58-62} ch-2 sps.

Rnds 5-15: Repeat Rnds 3 and 4, 5 times; then repeat Rnd 3 once **more**: {55-55}{59-59-63} sps.

Rnd 16: Ch 5, turn; dc in same st, skip next ch-2 sp, dc in next ch-3 sp, (ch 2, dc in same sp) twice, ★ skip next ch-4 sp, dc in next ch-3 sp, (ch 2, dc in same sp) twice; repeat from ★ around to last ch-2 sp, skip last ch-2 sp, dc in same st as first dc, ch 2; join with slip st to first dc: {56-56}{60-60-64} ch-2 sps.

Rnd 17: Ch 1, turn; sc in first ch-2 sp, ch 4, sc in next ch-2 sp, ★ ch 3, sc in next ch-2 sp, ch 4, sc in next ch-2 sp; repeat from ★ around, ch 1, sc in first sc to form last ch-2 sp.

Rnd 18: Ch 5, turn; dc in same st, skip next ch-4 sp, ★ dc in next ch-3 sp, (ch 2, dc in same sp) twice, skip next ch-4 sp; repeat from ★ around, dc in same st as first dc, ch 2; join with slip st to first dc.

Rnd 19: Repeat Rnd 17.

Rnd 20: Ch 5, turn; (dc, ch 2, dc) in last ch-2 sp made, ★ skip next ch-4 sp, dc in next ch-3 sp, (ch 2, dc in same sp) twice; repeat from ★ around to last ch-4 sp, skip last ch-4 sp, (dc, ch 2) twice in same st as first dc; join with slip st to first dc: {58-58}{62-62-66} ch-2 sps.

Rnd 21: Ch 5, turn; sc in next ch-2 sp, ch 3, sc in next ch-2 sp, ★ ch 4, sc in next ch-2 sp, ch 3, sc in next ch-2 sp; repeat from ★ around, ch 2; join with slip st to first dc.

Rnd 22: Ch 3, turn; skip next ch-2 sp, dc in next ch-3 sp, (ch 2, dc in same sp) twice, ★ skip next ch-4 sp, dc in next ch-3 sp, (ch 2, dc in same sp) twice; repeat from ★ around to last ch-2 sp, skip last ch-2 sp; join with slip st to first dc.

Rnd 23: Ch 5, turn; sc in next ch-2 sp, ch 3, sc in next ch-2 sp, ★ ch 4, sc in next ch-2 sp, ch 3, sc in next ch-2 sp; repeat from ★ around, ch 2; join with slip st to first dc.

Rnds 24-31: Repeat Rnds 16-23 once, then repeat Rnds 16 and 17 once **more**: {64-64}{68-68-72} sps.

Rnd 32: Ch 1, turn; 2 sc in last ch-2 sp made, 4 sc in next ch-4 sp, (3 sc in next ch-3 sp, 4 sc in next ch-4 sp) around, sc in same sp as first sc; join with slip st first sc, finish off.

Finishing

Sew Sleeves into Armholes, easing as necessary.

Sew side and underarm in one continuous seam.

Peasant Top

■■□□ **EASY**

Size	Finished Chest Measurement
Large	42" (106.5 cm)
Extra Large	48" (122 cm)
2X-Large	54" (137 cm)
3X-Large	56" (142 cm)
4X-Large	60" (152.5 cm)

Size Note: Instructions are written with sizes Large and Extra Large in the first set of braces { } and with sizes 2X-Large, 3X-Large, and 4X-Large in the second set of braces. Instructions will be easier to read if you circle all the numbers pertaining to your size. If only one number is given, it applies to all sizes.

MATERIALS

FINE 2

Fine Weight Yarn
[4 ounces, 335 yards
(113 grams, 306 meters) per skein]:
{6-6}{7-8-9} skeins
Crochet hooks,
 Sizes Large, Extra Large, 2X-Large, and 4X-Large:
  size F (3.75 mm) **or** size needed for gauge
 Size 3X-Large:
  size G (4 mm) **or** size needed for gauge
Safety pin
Tapestry needle

GAUGE

Sizes Large, Extra Large, 2X-Large, and 4X-Large:
In pattern, with smaller size hook,
18 sts (1 repeat) and 6 rows = 3" (7.5 cm)
Size 3X-Large:
In pattern, with larger size hook,
18 sts (1 repeat) and 6 rows = 3½" (9 cm)

Gauge Swatch:
Sizes Large, Extra Large, 2X-Large, and 4X-Large:
6¼" x 3" (16 cm x 7.5 cm)
With smaller size hook, ch 41.
Rows 1-6: Work same as Back.
Finish off.
Size 3X-Large:
7¼" x 3½" (18.5 cm x 9 cm)
With larger size hook, ch 41.
Rows 1-6: Work same as Back.
Finish off.

Top is worked beginning at the bottom of the Back, up and over the shoulders and down the Front.

Back
BODY
Ch {131-149}{167-149-185}.

Row 1 (Right side): Dc in eighth ch from hook **(skipped chs count as first dc, one ch-2 sp, and 2 skipped chs, now and throughout)**, ch 2, skip next 2 chs, dc in next ch, ch 2, skip next 2 chs, dc in next 4 chs, ★ (ch 2, skip next 2 chs, dc in next ch) 4 times, ch 2, skip next 2 chs, dc in next 4 chs; repeat from ★ across to last 6 chs, (ch 2, skip next 2 chs, dc in next ch) twice: {57-65}{73-65-81} dc and {35-40}{45-40-50} ch-2 sps.

Note: Loop a short piece of yarn around any stitch to mark Row 1 as **right** side.

Row 2: Ch 5 (counts as first dc plus ch 2, now and throughout), turn; dc in next dc, 2 dc in next ch-2 sp, dc in next dc, ch 5, skip next 2 dc, dc in next dc, 2 dc in next ch-2 sp, dc in next dc, ★ (ch 2, dc in next dc) 3 times, 2 dc in next ch-2 sp, dc in next dc, ch 5, skip next 2 dc, dc in next dc, 2 dc in next ch-2 sp, dc in next dc; repeat from ★ across to last 2 dc, (ch 2, dc in next dc) twice: {71-81}{91-81-101} dc and {28-32}{36-32-40} sps.

Row 3: Ch 5, turn; dc in next dc, 2 dc in next ch-2 sp, dc in next dc, ch 4, sc in center ch of next ch-5, ch 4, skip next 3 dc, dc in next dc, 2 dc in next ch-2 sp, dc in next dc, ★ ch 2, dc in next dc, 2 dc in next ch-2 sp, dc in next dc, ch 4, sc in center ch of next ch-5, ch 4, skip next 3 dc, dc in next dc, 2 dc in next ch-2 sp, dc in next dc; repeat from ★ across: {64-73}{82-73-91} sts and {21-24} {27-24-30} sps.

Instructions continued on page 14.

Row 4: Ch 9 (counts as first dc plus ch 6), turn; sc in next sc, ch 6, skip next 3 dc, dc in next dc, 2 dc in next ch-2 sp, dc in next dc, ★ ch 6, sc in next sc, ch 6, skip next 3 dc, dc in next dc, 2 dc in next ch-2 sp, dc in next dc; repeat from ★ across: {36-41}{46-41-51} sts and {14-16}{18-16-20} sps.

Row 5: Ch 5, turn; skip next 2 dc, dc in next dc, 3 dc in next ch-6 sp, ch 5, sc in next sc, ch 5, 3 dc in next ch-6 sp, dc in next dc, ★ ch 2, skip next 2 dc, dc in next dc, 3 dc in next ch-6 sp, ch 5, sc in next sc, ch 5, 3 dc in next ch-6 sp, dc in next dc; repeat from ★ across: {64-73}{82-73-91} sts and {21-24}{27-24-30} sps.

Row 6: Ch 5, turn; skip next 2 dc, dc in next dc, 3 dc in next ch-5 sp, ch 2, 3 dc in next ch-5 sp, dc in next dc, ch 2, skip next 2 dc, dc in next dc, ch 2, dc in next dc, ★ ch 2, skip next 2 dc, dc in next dc, 3 dc in next ch-5 sp, ch 2, 3 dc in next ch-5 sp, dc in next dc, ch 2, skip next 2 dc, dc in next dc, ch 2, dc in next dc; repeat from ★ across: {71-81}{91-81-101} dc and {28-32}{36-32-40} ch-2 sps.

Row 7: Ch 5, turn; (dc in next dc, ch 2) twice, skip next 2 dc, dc in next dc, 2 dc in next ch-2 sp, dc in next dc, ch 2, skip next 2 dc, dc in next dc, ★ (ch 2, dc in next dc) 3 times, skip next 2 dc, dc in next dc, 2 dc in next ch-2 sp, dc in next dc, ch 2, skip next 2 dc, dc in next dc; repeat from ★ across to last dc, ch 2, dc in last dc: {57-65}{73-65-81} dc and {35-40}{45-40-50} ch-2 sps.

Rows 8 thru {48-48}{48-42-48}: Repeat Rows 2-7, {6-6}{6-5-6} times; then repeat Rows 2-6 once more: {71-81}{91-81-101} dc and {28-32}{36-32-40} ch-2 sps.

SLEEVES AND YOKE

Slip loop from hook onto safety pin to prevent work from unraveling while working ch for second Sleeve, with **right** side facing, join yarn with slip st in first dc, ch {36-54}{54-54-72}; finish off.

Row 1: Slip loop from safety pin onto hook; ch {40-58}{58-58-76}, dc in eighth ch from hook, ch 2, skip next 2 chs, dc in next ch, ch 2, skip next 2 chs, dc in next 4 chs, † (ch 2, skip next 2 chs, dc in next ch) 4 times, ch 2, skip next 2 chs, dc in next 4 chs †; repeat from † to † {0-1}{1-1-2} time(s) **more (see Zeros, page 58)**, ch 2, skip next 2 chs, dc in next ch, ch 2, skip next 2 chs, dc in next dc, (ch 2, dc in next dc) twice, ch 2, skip next 2 dc, dc in next dc, 2 dc in next ch-2 sp, dc in next dc, ch 2, skip next 2 dc, dc in next dc, ★ (ch 2, dc in next dc) 3 times, ch 2, skip next 2 dc, dc in next dc, 2 dc in next ch-2 sp, dc in next dc, ch 2, skip next 2 dc, dc in next dc; repeat from ★ across to last dc, ch 2, dc in last dc, (ch 2, skip next 2 chs, dc in next ch) twice, ch 2, skip next 2 chs, dc in next 4 chs, repeat from † to † across to last 6 chs, (ch 2, skip next 2 chs, dc in next ch) twice: {89-113}{121-113-145} dc and {55-70}{75-70-90} ch-2 sps.

Rows 2 thru {12-12}{12-12-18}: Repeat Rows 2-7 of Body, {1-1}{1-1-2} time(s); then repeat Rows 2-6 once **more**; do **not** finish off.

Neck Opening
RIGHT SIDE

Row 1: Ch 5, turn; (dc in next dc, ch 2) twice, skip next 2 dc, dc in next dc, 2 dc in next ch-2 sp, dc in next dc, ch 2, skip next 2 dc, ★ (dc in next dc, ch 2) 4 times, skip next 2 dc, dc in next dc, 2 dc in next ch-2 sp, dc in next dc, ch 2, skip next 2 dc; repeat from ★ {2-3}{3-3-4} times **more**, dc in next dc, ch 2, dc in next dc, leave remaining sts unworked: {33-41}{41-41-49} dc and {20-25}{25-25-30} ch-2 sps.

Rows 2-18: Repeat Rows 2-7 of Body twice, then repeat Rows 2-6 once **more**; at end of Row 18, do **not** finish off, place loop from hook onto safety pin to keep piece from unraveling while working Left Side.

LEFT SIDE

Row 1: With **right** side facing, skip next {12-16}{20-16-24} ch-2 sps from Right Side and join yarn with dc in next dc; (ch 2, dc in next dc) twice, ch 2, skip next 2 dc, dc in next dc, 2 dc in next ch-2 sp, dc in next dc, ★ ch 2, skip next 2 dc, dc in next dc, (ch 2, dc in next dc) 3 times, ch 2, skip next 2 dc, dc in next dc, 2 dc in next ch-2 sp, dc in next dc; repeat from ★ across to last 4 dc, ch 2, skip next 2 dc, dc in next dc, ch 2, dc in last dc: {33-41}{41-41-49} dc and {20-25}{25-25-30} ch-2 sps.

Rows 2-18: Repeat Rows 2-7 of Body twice, then repeat Rows 2-6 once **more**; at end of Row 18, finish off.

Front

SLEEVES AND YOKE

Row 1: With **right** side facing, slip loop from safety pin onto hook, ch 5, (dc in next dc, ch 2) twice, skip next 2 dc, dc in next dc, 2 dc in next ch-2 sp, dc in next dc, † ch 2, skip next 2 dc, dc in next dc, (ch 2, dc in next dc) 3 times, ch 2, skip next 2 dc, dc in next dc, 2 dc in next ch-2 sp, dc in next dc †; repeat from † to † across to last 4 dc on Right Side Neck Opening, ch 2, skip next 2 dc, dc in next dc, ch 2, dc in last dc, ch {53-71}{89-71-107} (neck opening), (dc in next dc, ch 2) 3 times, skip next 2 dc, dc in next dc, 2 dc in next ch-2 sp, dc in next dc, repeat from † to † across to last 4 dc, ch 2, skip next 2 dc, dc in next dc, ch 2, dc in last dc.

Row 2: Ch 5, turn; dc in next dc, 2 dc in next ch-2 sp, dc in next dc, ch 5, skip next 2 dc, dc in next dc, 2 dc in next ch-2 sp, dc in next dc, † (ch 2, dc in next dc) 3 times, 2 dc in next ch-2 sp, dc in next dc, ch 5, skip next 2 dc, dc in next dc, 2 dc in next ch-2 sp, dc in next dc †; repeat from † to † across to within 2 ch-2 sps of Neck Opening, (ch 2, dc in next dc) twice, ch 2, skip next 2 chs, dc in next 4 chs, ch 5, skip next 2 chs, dc in next 4 chs, ★ (ch 2, skip next 2 chs, dc in next ch) twice, ch 2, skip next 2 chs, dc in next 4 chs, ch 5, skip next 2 chs, dc in next 4 chs; repeat from ★ across to last 5 chs, ch 2, skip next 2 chs, dc in next ch, ch 2, skip last 2 chs, dc in next dc, ch 2, dc in next dc, 2 dc in next ch-2 sp, dc in next dc, ch 5, skip next 2 dc, dc in next dc, 2 dc in next ch-2 sp, dc in next dc, repeat from † to † across to last 2 dc, (ch 2, dc in next dc) twice.

Rows 3 thru {13-13}{13-13-19}: Repeat Rows 3-7 of Body once; then repeat Rows 2-7 {1-1}{1-1-2} time(s) **more**.

Finish off.

Instructions continued on page 16.

BODY

Row 1: With **wrong** side facing, skip first {10-15}
{15-15-20} ch-2 sps and join yarn with dc in next dc;
ch 2, dc in next dc, 2 dc in next ch 2 sp, dc in next dc,
ch 5, skip next 2 dc, dc in next dc, 2 dc in next ch-2 sp,
dc in next dc, ★ (ch 2, dc in next dc) 3 times, 2 dc in
next ch 2 sp, dc in next dc, ch 5, skip next 2 dc, dc in
next dc, 2 dc in next ch-2 sp, dc in next dc; repeat from
★ across to last {12-17}{17-17-22} ch-2 sps, (ch 2, dc
in next dc) twice, leave remaining sts unworked: {57-65}
{73-65-81} dc and {35-40}{45-40-50} ch-2 sps.

Row 2: Ch 5, turn; dc in next dc, 2 dc in next ch-2 sp,
dc in next dc, ch 4, sc in center ch of next ch 5, ch 4,
skip next 3 dc, dc in next dc, 2 dc in next ch-2 sp, dc in
next dc, ★ ch 2, dc in next dc, 2 dc in next ch-2 sp, dc
in next dc, ch 4, sc in center ch of next ch-5, ch 4, skip
next 3 dc, dc in next dc, 2 dc in next ch-2 sp, dc in next
dc; repeat from ★ across: {64-73}{82-73-91} sts and
{21-24}{27-24-30} sps.

Row 3: Ch 9 **(counts as first dc plus ch 6)**, turn; sc
in next sc, ch 6, skip next 3 dc, dc in next dc, 2 dc in
next ch-2 sp, dc in next dc, ★ ch 6, sc in next sc, ch 6,
skip next 3 dc, dc in next dc, 2 dc in next ch-2 sp, dc in
next dc; repeat from ★ across: {36-41}{46-41-51} sts
and {14-16}{18-16-20} sps.

Row 4: Ch 5, turn; skip next 2 dc, dc in next dc,
3 dc in next ch-6 sp, ch 5, sc in next sc, ch 5, 3 dc in
next ch-6 sp, dc in next dc, ★ ch 2, skip next 2 dc,
dc in next dc, 3 dc in next ch-6 sp, ch 5, sc in next
sc, ch 5, 3 dc in next ch-6 sp, dc in next dc; repeat
from ★ across: {64-73}{82-73-91} sts and {21-24}
{27-24-30} sps.

Row 5: Ch 5, turn; skip next 2 dc, dc in next dc, 3 dc
in next ch-5 sp, ch 2, 3 dc in next ch-5 sp, dc in next
dc, ch 2, skip next 2 dc, dc in next dc, ch 2, dc in next
dc, ★ ch 2, skip next 2 dc, dc in next dc, 3 dc in next
ch-5 sp, ch 2, 3 dc in next ch-5 sp, dc in next dc, ch 2,
skip next 2 dc, dc in next dc, ch 2, dc in next dc; repeat
from ★ across: {71-81}{91-81-101} dc and {28-32}
{36-32-40} ch-2 sps.

Row 6: Ch 5, turn; (dc in next dc, ch 2) twice, skip next 2 dc, dc in next dc, 2 dc in next ch-2 sp, dc in next dc, ch 2, skip next 2 dc, dc in next dc, ★ (ch 2, dc in next dc) 3 times, ch 2, skip next 2 dc, dc in next dc, 2 dc in next ch-2 sp, dc in next dc, ch 2, skip next 2 dc, dc in next dc; repeat from ★ across to last dc, ch 2, dc in last dc: {57-65}{73-65-81} dc and {35-40} {45-40-50} ch-2 sps.

Row 7: Ch 5, turn; dc in next dc, 2 dc in next ch-2 sp, dc in next dc, ch 5, skip next 2 dc, dc in next dc, 2 dc in next ch-2 sp, dc in next dc, ★ (ch 2, dc in next dc) 3 times, 2 dc in next ch-2 sp, dc in next dc, ch 5, skip next 2 dc, dc in next dc, 2 dc in next ch-2 sp, dc in next dc; repeat from ★ across to last 2 dc, (ch 2, dc in next dc) twice: {71-81}{91-81-101} dc and {28-32} {36-32-40} sps.

Rows 7 thru {48-48}{48-42-48}: Repeat Rows 2-7, {6-6}{6-5-6} times; then repeat Rows 2-6 once **more**: {57-65}{73-65-81} dc and {35-40} {45-40-50} ch-2 sps.

Finish off.

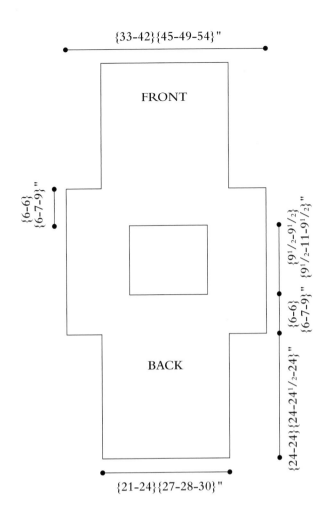

Finishing

Sew side and Sleeve in one continuous seam.

Make a 80" (203 cm) long twisted cord tie *(see Twisted Cord, page 59)*.

Using photo as a guide, weave cord through sps along Neck Opening.

.

Stole

Finished Size:
16¹/₂" x 84" (42 cm x 213 cm)

MATERIALS

Light Weight Yarn
[2.2 ounces, 102 yards
(65 grams, 93 meters) per ball]:
    18 balls
Crochet hook, size K (6.5 mm) **or**
    size needed for gauge
Assorted seed and pearl beads
Beading needle and thread

GAUGE: In pattern, (sc, ch 1, dc) 7 times and 13 rows = 4" (10 cm)

Gauge Swatch: 4¹/₂" (11.5 cm) square
Ch 24.
Work same as Body for 13 rows: 15 sts and 7 ch–1 sps.
Finish off.

Body

Ch 90.

Row 1 (Right side): (Sc, ch 1, dc) in third ch from hook, ★ skip next 2 chs, (sc, ch 1, dc) in next ch; repeat from ★ across to last 3 chs, skip next 2 chs, sc in last ch: 59 sts and 29 ch-1 sps.

Note: Loop a short piece of yarn around any stitch to mark Row 1 as **right** side.

Row 2: Ch 2, turn; (sc, ch 1, dc) in next ch–1 sp and in each ch–1 sp across, sc in top of turning ch.

Repeat Row 2 until Body measures approximately 84" (213 cm) from beginning ch, ending by working a **right** side row.

Finish off.

Beaded Fringe

Thread beading needle with beading thread and secure thread to first stitch on last row; then thread a 3" (7.5 cm) assortment of beads, making sure that the last bead is a seed bead. Skip the last seed bead and thread needle back through all of the other beads, then secure thread to the Body by running it through several stitches.

Using photo as a guide, repeat Beaded Fringe across both short edges of Body.

Motif Bolero

●■□□ **EASY**

Size	Finished Chest Measurement
Large	40" (101.5 cm)
Extra Large	44" (112 cm)
2X-Large	50" (127 cm)
3X-Large	55" (139.5 cm)

Size Note: Yarn amounts are given for size Large with sizes Extra Large, 2X-Large, and 3X-Large in braces { }. Follow the same instructions for all sizes; finished measurements are obtained by using a different size hook as indicated in Materials.

MATERIALS

Light Weight Yarn 🔳**3** LIGHT
[3.52 ounces, 232 yards
(100 grams, 212 meters) per skein]:
   5{5-6-6} skeins
Crochet hook,
   Sizes Large and 2X-Large:
      size D (3.25 mm) **or** size needed for gauge
   Sizes Extra Large and 3X-Large:
      F (3.75 mm) **or** size needed for gauge
1/4" (7 mm) wide Grosgrain ribbon
Sew-on hook and eye closures - 2 sets
3/4" (19 mm) Button or desired button
Sewing needle and matching thread

GAUGE SWATCH: 5{5½-5-5½} square
Work same as First Motif.

STITCH GUIDE

> **SMALL PICOT**
> Ch 3, slip st in top of last st made.

First Motif

Rnd 1 (Right side)**:** Ch 2, sc in second ch from hook, (ch 6, sc in same ch) 7 times, ch 3, dc in first sc to form last ch-6 sp: 8 ch-6 sps.

Note: Loop a short piece of yarn around any stitch to mark Rnd 1 as **right** side.

Rnd 2: Ch 1, sc in last ch-6 sp made, ch 5, (sc in next ch-6 sp, ch 5) around; join with slip st to first sc.

Rnd 3: Ch 6 (**counts as first dc plus ch 3, now and throughout**), dc in same st, ch 3, (dc, ch 3) twice in each sc around; join with slip st to first dc: 16 ch-3 sps.

Rnd 4: (Slip st, ch 1, sc) in first ch-3 sp, 10 dc in next ch-3 sp, sc in next ch-3 sp, ★ (ch 5, sc in next ch-3 sp) twice, 10 dc in next ch-3 sp, sc in next ch-3 sp; repeat from ★ 2 times **more**, ch 5, sc in next ch-3 sp, ch 2, dc in first sc to form last ch-5 sp: 52 sts and 8 ch-5 sps.

Rnd 5: Ch 1, sc in last ch-5 sp made, ch 1, (dc in next dc, ch 1) 10 times, sc in next ch-5 sp, ★ ch 5, sc in next ch-5 sp, ch 1, (dc in next dc, ch 1) 10 times, sc in next ch-5 sp; repeat from ★ 2 times **more**, ch 2, dc in first sc to form last ch-5 sp: 48 sts and 48 sps.

Rnd 6: Ch 1, sc in last ch-5 sp made, ★ † ch 5, (sc in next 2 ch-1 sps, work small Picot) twice, sc in next ch-1 sp, ch 9, slip st in top of last sc made, sc in next 2 ch-1 sps, ch 4, slip st in fifth ch of last ch-9 made, ch 4, slip st in top of last sc made, sc in next ch-1 sp, work Small Picot, sc in next 2 ch-1 sps, work small Picot, sc in next ch-1 sp, ch 5 †, sc in next ch-5 sp; repeat from ★ 2 times **more**, then repeat from † to † once; join with slip st to first sc, finish off.

Additional Motifs

Make 31 for sizes Large and Extra Large and make 34 for sizes 2X-Large and 3X-Large.

Work same as First Motif through Rnd 5: 48 sts and 48 sps.

The method used to connect the Motifs is a no-sew joining also known as "join-as-you-go." After the First Motif is made, each remaining Motif is worked to the last round, then crocheted together as the last round is worked.

Join Motifs as indicated on diagram, page 24, using One or Two Side Joining. Holding pieces with **wrong** sides together, work a slip stitch into space as indicated. When working into a corner space that has been previously joined, work into the joining slip stitch.

Instructions continued on page 22.

ONE SIDE JOINING

Rnd 6 (Joining rnd)**:** Ch 1, sc in last ch-5 sp made, ch 5, (sc in next 2 ch-1 sps, work Small Picot) twice, sc in next ch-1 sp, ★ ch 9, slip st in last sc made, sc in next 2 ch-1 sps, ch 4, slip st in fifth ch of last ch-9 made, ch 4, slip st in top of last sc made, sc in next ch-1 sp, work Small Picot, sc in next 2 ch-1 sps, work Small Picot, sc in next ch-1 sp, ch 5, sc in next ch-5 sp, ch 5, (sc in next 2 ch-1 sps, work Small Picot) twice, sc in next ch-1 sp; repeat from ★ once **more**, ch 9, slip st in top of last sc made, sc in next 2 ch-1 sps, ch 4, slip st in fifth ch of last ch-9 made, slip st in corresponding sp on **adjacent Motif**, ch 4, slip st in top of last sc made on **new Motif**, sc in next ch-1 sp, † ch 1, slip st in next Small Picot on **adjacent Motif**, ch 1, slip st in top of last sc made on **new Motif**, sc in next 2 ch-1 sps, ch 1, slip st in next Small Picot on **adjacent Motif**, ch 1, slip st in top of last sc made on **new Motif**, sc in next ch-1 sp †, ch 2, slip st in next ch-5 sp on **adjacent Motif**, ch 2, sc in next ch-5 sp on **new Motif**, ch 2, slip st in next ch-5 sp on **adjacent Motif**, ch 2, sc in next 2 ch-1 sps on **new Motif**, repeat from † to † once, ch 4, slip st in corresponding sp on **adjacent Motif**, ch 4, slip st in top of last sc made, sc in next 2 ch-1 sps, ch 4, slip st in ch after last joining slip st, ch 4, sc in next ch-1 sp, work Small Picot, sc in next 2 ch-1 sps, work Small Picot, sc in last ch-1 sp, ch 5; join with slip st to first sc, finish off.

TWO SIDE JOINING

Rnd 6 (Joining rnd)**:** Ch 1, sc in last ch-5 sp made, ch 5, (sc in next 2 ch-1 sps, work Small Picot) twice, sc in next ch-1 sp, ch 9, slip st in top of last sc made, sc in next 2 ch-1 sps, ch 4, slip st in fifth ch of last ch-9 made, ch 4, slip st in top of last sc made, sc in next ch-1 sp, work Small Picot, sc in next 2 ch-1 sps, work Small Picot, sc in next ch-1 sp, ch 5, sc in next ch-5 sp, ch 5, sc in next 2 ch-1 sps, work Small Picot, sc in next ch-1 sp, ch 5, sc in next ch-5 sp, ch 5, (sc in next 2 ch-1 sps, work Small Picot) twice, sc in next ch-1 sp, ♥ ch 9, slip st in last sc made, sc in next 2 ch-1 sps, ch 4, slip st in fifth ch of last ch-9 made, slip st in corresponding sp on **adjacent Motif**, ch 4, slip st in top of last sc made on **new Motif**, sc in next ch-1 sp ♥, ★ † ch 1, slip st in next Small Picot on **adjacent Motif**, ch 1, slip st in top of last sc made on **new Motif**, sc in next 2 ch-1 sps, ch 1, slip st in next Small Picot on **adjacent Motif**, ch 1, slip st in top of

last sc made on **new Motif**, sc in next ch-1 sp †, ch 2, slip st in next ch-5 sp on **adjacent Motif**, ch 2, sc in next ch-5 sp on **new Motif**, ch 2, slip st in next ch-5 sp on **adjacent Motif**, ch 2, sc in next 2 ch-1 sps on **new Motif**, repeat from † to † once, repeat from ♥ to ♥ once; repeat from ★ once **more**, work Small Picot, sc in next 2 ch-1 sps, work Small Picot, sc in last ch-1 sp, ch 5; join with slip st to first sc, finish off.

Triangle

Foundation Rnd: Ch 2, sc in second ch from hook, (ch 6, sc in same ch) 4 times, ch 3, dc in same ch to form last ch-6 sp: 5 ch-6 sps.

Begin working in rows.

Row 1 (Right side)**:** Ch 1, turn; sc in last ch-6 sp made, (ch 5, sc in next ch-6 sp) across; do **not** join: 5 sc and 4 ch-5 sps.

Note: Mark Row 1 as **right** side.

Row 2: Ch 6, turn; (dc, ch 3) twice in each of next 3 sc, dc in last sc: 7 ch-3 sps.

Row 3: Ch 3 (counts as first dc, now and throughout), turn; 4 dc in next ch-3 sp, sc in next ch-3 sp, (ch 5, sc) twice in next ch-3 sp, 10 dc in next ch-3 sp, (sc, ch 5) twice in next ch-3 sp, sc in next ch-3 sp, 4 dc in next ch-3 sp, dc in last dc: 26 sts and 4 ch-5 sps.

Row 4: Ch 4 (counts as first dc plus ch 1, now and throughout), turn; (dc in next dc, ch 1) 4 times, sc in next ch-5 sp, ch 5, sc in next ch-5 sp, ch 1, (dc in next dc, ch 1) 10 times, sc in next ch-5 sp, ch 5, sc in next ch-5 sp, (ch 1, dc in next dc) across: 24 sts and 23 sps.

Row 5 (Joining row)**:** Ch 1, turn; sc in first ch-1 sp, ch 4, slip st in corresponding sp on **adjacent Motif**, ch 4, slip st in top of last sc made on **new Motif**, sc in next ch-1 sp, † ch 1, slip st in next Small Picot on **adjacent Motif**, ch 1, slip st in top of last sc made on **new Motif**, sc in next 2 ch-1 sps, ch 1, slip st in next Small Picot on adjacent Motif, ch 1, slip st in top of last sc made on new Motif, sc in next ch-1 sp †, ch 2, slip st in next ch-5 sp on adjacent Motif, ch 2, sc in next ch-5 sp on new Motif, ch 2, slip st in next ch-5 sp on adjacent Motif, ch 2, sc in next 2 ch-1 sps on new Motif, repeat from † to † once, ch 4, slip st in corresponding sp on adjacent Motif, ch 4, slip st in top of last sc made on new Motif, sc in next 2 ch-1 sps, ch 4, slip st in fifth ch of last ch-9 made, slip st in corresponding sp on adjacent Motif, ch 4, slip st in top of last sc made on new Motif, sc in next ch-1 sp, repeat from † to † once, ch 2, slip st in next ch-5 sp on adjacent Motif, ch 2, sc in next ch-5 sp on new Motif, ch 2, slip st in next ch-5 sp on adjacent Motif, ch 2, sc in next 2 ch-1 sps on new Motif, repeat from † to † once, ch 4, slip st in next sp on adjacent Motif, ch 4, slip st in top of last sc made on new Motif, sc in last dc; finish off.

Left Two-Thirds Motif

SIZES 2X-LARGE AND 3X-LARGE ONLY

Row 1: Ch 6, sc in sixth ch from hook (**5 skipped chs count as first dc plus ch 2**), (ch 6, sc in same ch) 3 times, ch 2, dc in same ch: 5 sps.

Row 2 (Right side): Ch 1, turn; sc in first dc, ch 5, (sc in next ch-6 sp, ch 5) 4 times, sc in last dc: 5 ch-5 sps.

Note: Mark Row 2 as **right** side.

Row 3: Ch 6, turn; (dc, ch 3) twice in same sc and in each of next 4 sc: 11 dc and 10 ch-3 sps.

Row 4: Ch 3, turn; 4 dc in next ch-3 sp, sc in next ch-3 sp, ★ (ch 5, sc in next ch-3 sp) twice, 10 dc in next ch-3 sp, sc in next ch-3 sp; repeat from ★ once **more**, ch 5, sc in last dc: 33 sts and 5 ch-5 sps.

Row 5: Ch 5, turn; sc in next ch-5 sp, ★ ch 1, (dc in next dc, ch 1) 10 times, sc in next ch-5 sp, ch 5, sc in next ch-5 sp; repeat from ★ once **more**, (ch 1, dc in next dc) 5 times: 31 sts and 30 sps.

Row 6 (Joining row): Ch 1, turn; sc in first ch-1 sp, ch 4, slip st in next corresponding sp on adjacent Motif, ch 4, slip st in top of last sc made on new Motif, ♥ sc in next ch-1 sp, † ch 1, slip st in next Small Picot on adjacent Motif, ch 1, slip st in top of last sc made on new Motif, sc in next 2 ch-1 sps, ch 1, slip st in next Small Picot on adjacent Motif, ch 1, slip st in top of last sc made on new Motif, sc in next ch-1 sp †, ch 2, slip st in corresponding ch-5 sp on adjacent Motif, ch 2, sc in next ch-5 sp on new Motif, ch 2, slip st in next ch-5 sp on adjacent Motif, ch 2, sc in next 2 ch-1 sps on new Motif, repeat from † to † once, ♥ ch 4, slip st in next sp on adjacent Motif, ch 4, slip st in top of last sc made on new Motif, sc in next 2 ch-1 sps, ch 4, slip st in next ch after joining slip st and in next sp on adjacent Motif, ch 4, slip st in top of last sc made on new Motif, repeat ♥ to ♥ once, slip st in corresponding sp on adjacent Motif, ch 4, slip st in top of last sc made on new Motif, sc in next 2 ch-1 sps, ch 4, slip st in next ch after last joining slip st, ch 4, slip st in top of last sc made, sc in next ch-1 sp, work Small Picot, sc in next 2 ch-1 sps, work Small Picot, sc in next ch-1 sp, ch 5, sc in last dc; finish off.

Instructions continued on page 24.

SIZES LARGE and EXTRA LARGE

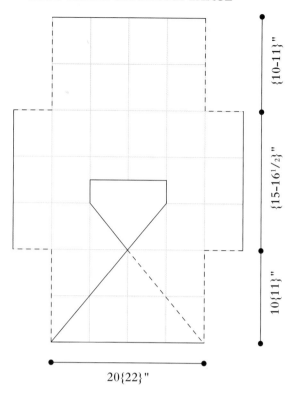

{10-11}"

{15-16¹/₂}"

10{11}"

20{22}"

SIZES 2X-LARGE and 3X-LARGE

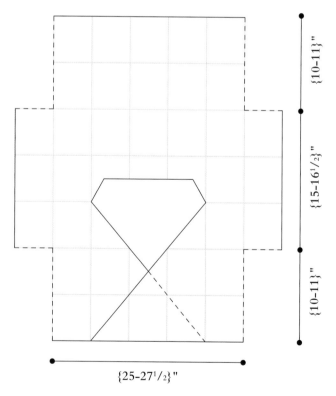

{10-11}"

{15-16¹/₂}"

{10-11}"

{25-27¹/₂}"

*Note: Dashed lines at sides and underarms
indicate joined motifs.*

Half Motif

SIZES 2X-LARGE AND 3X-LARGE ONLY

Row 1: Ch 6, sc in sixth ch from hook (**5 skipped chs count as first dc plus ch 2**), (ch 6, dc in same ch) 4 times, ch 2, dc in same ch: 6 sps.

Row 2 (Right side)**:** Ch 5 (**counts as first dc plus ch 2, now and throughout**), turn; sc in next ch-6 sp, (ch 5, sc in next ch-6 sp) 3 times, ch 2, dc in last dc: 6 sts and 5 sps.

Note: Mark Row 2 as **right** side.

Row 3: Ch 3, turn; (dc, ch 3) twice in each of next 3 sc, (dc, ch 3, dc) in next sc, dc in last dc: 10 dc and 7 ch-3 sps.

Row 4: Ch 1, turn; sc in first dc, ch 5, sc in next ch-3 sp, 10 dc in next ch-3 sp, sc in next ch-3 sp, (ch 5, sc in next ch-3 sp) twice, 10 dc in next ch-3 sp, sc in next ch-3 sp, ch 5, skip next dc, sc in last dc: 27 sts and 4 ch-5 sps.

Row 5: Ch 5, turn; sc in next ch-5 sp, ch 1, (dc in next dc, ch 1) 10 times, sc in next ch-5 sp, ch 5, sc in next ch-5 sp, ch 1, (dc in next dc, ch 1) 10 times, sc in next ch-5 sp, ch 2, dc in last sc: 26 sts and 25 sps.

Row 6 (Joining row)**:** Ch 1, turn; sc in first dc, ch 2, slip st in corresponding ch-5 sp on **adjacent Motif**, ch 2, sc in next 2 ch-1 sps **new Motif**, † ch 1, slip st in next Small Picot on **adjacent Motif**, ch 1, slip st in top of last sc made on **new Motif**, sc in next 2 ch-1 sps, ch 1, slip st in next Small Picot on **adjacent Motif**, ch 1, slip st in top of last sc made on **new Motif**, sc in next ch-1 sp †, ch 4, slip st in corresponding sp on **adjacent Motif**, ch 4, slip st in top of last sc made on **new Motif**, sc in next 2 ch-1 sps, ch 4, slip st in next ch after last joining slip st and in next sp on **adjacent Motif**, ch 4, slip st in top of last sc made on **new Motif**, sc in next ch-1 sp, repeat from † to † once, ch 2, slip st in next ch-5 sp on **adjacent Motif**, ch 2, sc in next ch-5 sp on **new Motif**, ch 2, slip st in next ch-5 sp on **adjacent Motif**, ch 2, sc in next 2 ch-1 sps on **new Motif**, repeat from

† to † once, ch 4, slip st in corresponding sp on **adjacent Motif**, ch 4, slip st in top of last sc made on **new Motif**, sc in next 2 ch-1 sps, ch 4, slip st in ch after last joining st, ch 4, slip st in top of last sc made, sc in next ch-1 sp, work Small Pioct, sc in next 2 ch-1 sps, work Small Picot, sc in next ch-1 sp, ch 5, sc in last dc; finish off.

Right Two-Thirds Motif

SIZES 2X-LARGE AND 3X-LARGE ONLY

Rows 1 and 2: Work same as Left Two-Thirds Motif: 5 ch-5 sps.

Row 3: Ch 6, turn; dc in same st, ch 3, (dc, ch 3) twice in each of next 3 sc, (dc, ch 3, dc, ch 3, dc) in last sc: 11 dc and 10 ch-3 sps.

Row 4: Ch 1, turn; sc in first dc, ch 5, sc in next ch-3 sp, ★ 10 dc in next ch-3 sp, sc in next ch-3 sp, (ch 5, sc in next ch-3 sp) twice; repeat from ★ once **more**, 4 dc in next ch-3 sp, dc in last dc: 33 sts and 5 ch-5 sps.

Row 5: Ch 4, turn; (dc in next dc, ch 1) 4 times, sc in next ch-5 sp, ★ ch 5, sc in next ch-5 sp, ch 1, (dc in next dc, ch 1) 10 times, sc in next ch-5 sp; repeat from ★ once **more**, ch 2, dc in last sc: 31 sts and 30 sps.

Row 6 (Joining row): Ch 1, turn; sc in first ch-1 sp, ★ ch 2, slip st in corresponding ch-5 sp on **adjacent Motif**, ch 2, sc in next 2 ch-1 sps on **new Motif**, † ch 1, slip st in next Small Picot on **adjacent Motif**, ch 1, slip st in top of last sc made on **new Motif,** sc in next 2 ch-1 sps, ch 1, slip in next Small Picot on **adjacent Motif**, ch 1, slip st in top of last sc made on **new Motif**, sc in next ch-1 sp †, ch 4, slip st in next sp on **adjacent Motif**, ch 4, slip st in top of last sc made on **new Motif**, sc in next 2 ch-1 sps, ch 4, slip st in ch after last joining slip st and in next sp on **adjacent Motif**, ch 4, slip st in top of last sc made on **new Motif**, sc in next ch-1 sp, repeat from † to † once, ch 2, slip st in next ch-5 sp on **adjacent Motif**, ch 2, sc in next ch-5 sp on **new Motif**; repeat from ★ once **more**, ch 2, slip st in next ch-5 sp

on **adjacent Motif**, ch 2, sc in next 2 ch-1 sps on **new Motif**, repeat from † to † once, ch 4, slip st in next sp on **adjacent Motif**, ch 4, slip st in top of last sc made on **new Motif**; finish off.

Finishing
BAND

Rnd 1: With **right** side facing, join yarn with sc in any st *(see Joining With Sc, page 58)*; sc evenly around entire piece increasing and decreasing as needed to keep piece lying flat; join with slip st to first sc.

Rnds 2-6: Ch 1, turn; sc in same st and in each sc around increasing and decreasing as needed to keep piece lying flat; join with slip st to first sc.

Finish off.

Hand sew grosgrain ribbon along **wrong** side of entire Band.

Sew button to **right** side of left front at corner.

Sew one hook half to **wrong** side of left front at corner.

Sew second hook half to **right** side of right front at corner.

Lay piece on a flat surface with left front over right front. Sew eye halves opposite from the hooks.

Felted Handbag

□■□□ EASY

Finished Size: Approximately
14" wide x 6" deep x 13¹/₂" high
(35.5 cm x 15 cm x 34.5 cm) after felting

MATERIALS

MEDIUM 4

Medium Weight Wool Yarn
[3.5 ounces, 220 yards
(100 grams, 201 meters) per hank]:
  Blue - 2 hanks
  Turquoise - 2 hanks
  Purple - 2 hanks
Crochet hook, size G (4 mm) **or** size needed
  for gauge
Plastic canvas 11" x 14" (28 cm x 35.5 cm) sheets - 3
Fabric - 36" x 45" (91.5 cm x 114.5 cm) piece
  for lining
Bag clasp
Set of bag feet
Handles - 2

GAUGE: 15 hdc and 12 rows = 4" (10 cm)

Gauge Swatch: 4" (10 cm) square
Ch 16.
Row 1: Hdc in second ch from hook and in each ch
across: 15 hdc.
Rows 2-12: Ch 1, turn; hdc in first hdc and in each hdc
across.
Finish off.

When changing colors *(Fig. 4, page 59)*, keep unused
color on **wrong** side of work. When working a large
area, work over unused color every fourth stitch, holding
yarn with normal tension; do **not** cut yarn until color is
no longer needed.

Base

With Blue, ch 73.

Row 1: Hdc in second ch from hook and in each ch
across: 72 hdc.

Rows 2-24: Ch 1, turn; hdc in first hdc and in each hdc
across; at end of Row 24, do **not** finish off.

Body

Rnd 1 (Right side)**:** Ch 1, turn; hdc in first hdc and
in each hdc across, place marker around last hdc made;
work 36 hdc evenly spaced across end of rows, place
marker around last hdc made; working in free loops of
beginning ch *(Fig. 3b, page 59)*, hdc in each ch across,
place marker around last hdc made; work 36 hdc evenly
spaced across end of rows; join with slip st to first hdc:
216 hdc.

Chart

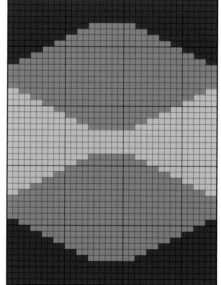

Rnd 48

Rnd 1

Note: Loop a short piece of yarn around any stitch to mark Rnd 1 as **right** side.

Rnds 2–48: Ch 1, turn; hdc in first hdc and in each hdc around following Chart; join with slip st to first hdc; at end of Row 48, finish off.

Felting

Set your top-loading washing machine for a HOT wash and COLD rinse cycle. Add about a tablespoon of detergent to the wash. Place the crocheted project in a tight-mesh lingerie or sweater bag and toss into the machine. Throw in an **old** pair of jeans to speed up the felting process (the more agitation, the better). Check every 2–3 minutes during the wash cycle to keep an eye on size and shrinkage of the project. A properly felted project has shrunk to the desired size and the stitches are hard to see. When checking, you may want to wear rubber gloves to protect your hands from the hot water. Once it's felted, remove it from the machine and allow the wash water to spin out. Put the project back in the washer for the cold rinse.

Roll the felted item in a towel and gently squeeze out the excess water. Don't wring the towel as that may set in permanent creases. Form it into the size and shape by pinning to a blocking board, pulling top edge of one side to form tab for clasp. Let your project air dry even though it may take several days.

Finishing

Attach feet to Base of bag. Attach clasp to center of top edge, following instructions on package. Using photo as a guide, attach handles. Cut plastic canvas to size of Base and each long side. Sew plastic canvas to inside of bag. Line bag as desired.

A-Line Vest

Size	Finished Chest Measurement
Extra Large	43½" (110.5 cm)
2X-Large	49" (124.5 cm)
3X-Large	56" (142 cm)
4X-Large	61" (155 cm)

Size Note: Instructions are for size Extra Large with sizes 2X-Large, 3X-Large, and 4X-Large in braces { }. Instructions will be easier to read if you circle all the numbers pertaining to your size. If only one number is given, it applies to all sizes.

MATERIALS

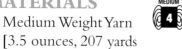

Medium Weight Yarn
[3.5 ounces, 207 yards
(100 grams, 188 meters) per skein]:
   Brown - 6{7-8-9} skeins
   Rose - 1 skein
Crochet hooks, sizes F (3.75 mm) **and** G (4 mm) **or**
   sizes needed for gauge
Yarn needle
Sewing needle and matching thread
⅞" (22 mm) Buttons - 4
Pins

GAUGE: In pattern, using larger size hook,
      15 sts = 4" (10 cm); 8 rows = 3½" (9 cm)
      Each Motif = 4" (10 cm) square

Gauge Swatch: 4¼" (10.75 cm) square
With larger size hook and Brown, ch 18.
Row 1: Dc in fouth ch from hook and in each ch across: 16 sts.
Row 2: Ch 1, turn; (sc, 2 dc) in first dc, ★ skip next 2 dc, (sc, 2 dc) in next dc; repeat from ★ across to last 3 dc, skip next 2 dc, sc in last dc.

Row 3: Ch 3 (**counts as first dc**), turn; dc in next st and in each st across.
Rows 4-10: Repeat Rows 2 and 3, 3 times; then repeat Row 2 once **more**.
Finish off.

STITCH GUIDE

> **TREBLE CROCHET** (*abbreviated tr*)
> YO twice, insert hook in st indicated, YO and pull up a loop (4 loops on hook), (YO and draw through 2 loops on hook) 3 times.
> **DECREASE** (uses next 3 sts)
> ★ YO, insert hook in **next** st, YO and pull up a loop, YO and draw through 2 loops on hook; repeat from ★ 2 times **more**, YO and draw through all 4 loops on hook (**counts as one dc**).
> **SMALL PICOT**
> Ch 3, slip st in third ch from hook.
> **LARGE PICOT**
> Ch 5, slip st in third ch from hook.

Vest is worked lengthwise from side to side. Row gauge is very important. The Back Panel uses a "join-as-you-go" method to join Motifs.

Left Body

FRONT

With larger size hook and Brown, ch 54.

Row 1 (Right side): Dc in fourth ch from hook (**3 skipped chs count as first dc**) and in each ch across to last ch, 4 dc in last ch: 55 dc.

Note: Loop a short piece of yarn around first dc to mark **right** side.

Row 2: Ch 7, turn; sc in second ch from hook and next 3 chs, hdc in next 5 sts, 2 dc in next dc, ★ skip next 2 dc, (sc, 2 dc) in next dc; repeat from ★ across to last 3 dc, skip next 2 dc, sc in last dc: 60 sts.

Row 3: Ch 3 **(counts as first dc, now and throughout)**, turn; dc in next st and in each st across to last sc, 4 dc in last sc: 63 dc.

Row 4: Ch 10, turn; sc in second ch from hook and next 5 chs, hdc in next 6 sts, (sc, 2 dc) in next dc, ★ skip next 2 dc, (sc, 2 dc) in next dc; repeat from ★ across to last 2 dc, skip next dc, sc in last dc: 73 sts.

Row 5 (Increase row)**:** Ch 3, turn; dc in next st and in each st across to last sc, 4 dc in last sc: 76 dc.

Row 6 (Increase row)**:** Ch 10, turn; sc in second ch from hook and next 5 chs, hdc in next 6 sts, (sc, 2 dc) in next dc, ★ skip next 2 dc, (sc, 2 dc) in next dc; repeat from ★ across to last 3 dc, skip next 2 dc, sc in last dc: 85 sts.

Rows 7-9: Repeat Rows 5 and 6 once, then repeat Row 5 once **more**: 100 sts.

Row 10: Ch 13, turn; sc in second ch from hook and next 6 chs, hdc in next 8 sts, (sc, 2 dc) in next dc, ★ skip next 2 dc, (sc, 2 dc) in next dc; repeat from ★ across to last 3 dc, skip next 2 dc, sc in last dc: 112 sts.

Row 11: Ch 3, turn; dc in next st and in each st across.

Row 12: Ch 1, turn; (sc, 2 dc) in first dc, ★ skip next 2 dc, (sc, 2 dc) in next dc; repeat from ★ across to last 3 dc, skip next 2 dc, sc in last dc.

Rows 13 thru 18{20-22-24}: Repeat Rows 11 and 12, 3{4-5-6} times.

Instructions continued on page 30.

ARMHOLE SHAPING

Row 1: Ch 3, turn; dc in next 81sts, decrease, leave remaining sts unworked: 83 dc.

Row 2: Ch 1, turn; skip first dc, (sc, 2 dc) in next dc, ★ skip next 2 dc, (sc, 2 dc) in next dc; repeat from ★ across to last 3 dc, skip next 2 dc, sc in last dc: 82 sts.

Row 3: Ch 3, turn; dc in next st and in each st across to last 3 sts, decrease: 80 dc.

Row 4: Ch 1, turn; skip first dc, (sc, 2 dc) in next dc, ★ skip next 2 dc, (sc, 2 dc) in next dc; repeat from ★ across to last 3 dc, skip next 2 dc, sc in last dc: 79 sts.

Row 5: Ch 3, turn; dc in next st and in each st across.

Row 6: Ch 1, turn; (sc, 2 dc) in first dc, ★ skip next 2 dc, (sc, 2 dc) in next dc; repeat from ★ across to last 3 dc, skip next 2 dc, sc in last dc.

Rows 7 thru 10{12-16-18}: Repeat Rows 5 and 6, 2{3-5-6} times; do **not** finish off.

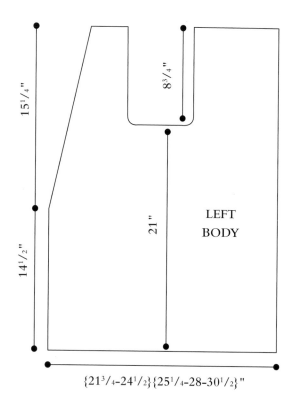

15¼"

8¾"

14½"

21"

LEFT BODY

{21³/₄-24½}{25¼-28-30½}"

BACK

Row 1: Ch 3, turn; dc in next st and in each st across to last sc, 2 dc in last sc: 80 dc.

Row 2: Ch 1, turn; 2 sc in first dc, (sc, 2 dc) in next dc, ★ skip next 2 dc, (sc, 2 dc) in next dc; repeat from ★ across to last 3 dc, skip next 2 dc, sc in last dc: 81 sts.

Row 3: Ch 3, turn; dc in next st and in each st across to last sc, 2 dc in last sc: 82 dc.

Row 4: Ch 31, turn; (sc, 2 dc) in second ch from hook, ★ skip next 2 sts, (sc, 2 dc) in next st; repeat from ★ across to last 3 dc, skip next 2 dc, sc in last dc: 112 sts.

Row 5: Ch 3, turn; dc in next st and in each st across.

Row 6: Ch 1, turn; (sc, 2 dc) in first dc, ★ skip next 2 dc, (sc, 2 dc) in next dc; repeat from ★ across to last 3 dc, skip next 2 dc, sc in last dc.

Rows 7 thru 21{23-25-27}: Repeat Rows 5 and 6, 7{8-9-10} times, then repeat Row 5 once **more**.

Finish off.

Right Body

BACK

With larger size hook and Brown, ch 113.

Row 1: (Sc, 2 dc) in second ch from hook, ★ skip next 2 chs, (sc, 2 dc) in next ch; repeat from ★ across to last 3 chs, skip next 2 chs, sc in last ch: 112 sts.

Row 2 (Right side): Ch 3, turn; dc in next st and in each st across.

Note: Mark Row 2 as **right** side.

Row 3: Ch 1, turn; (sc, 2 dc) in first dc, ★ skip next 2 dc, (sc, 2 dc) in next dc; repeat from ★ across to last 3 dc, skip next 2 dc, sc in last dc.

Row 4: Ch 3, turn; dc in next st and in each st across.

Rows 5 thru 17{19-21-23}: Repeat Rows 3 and 4, 6{7-8-9} times; then repeat Row 3 once **more**, do **not** finish off.

ARMHOLE SHAPING

Work same as Left Body Armhole Shaping; do **not** finish off.

FRONT

Row 1: Ch 3, turn; dc in next st and in each st across to last sc, 2 dc in last sc: 80 dc.

Row 2: Ch 1, turn; 2 sc in first dc, (sc, 2 dc) in next dc, ★ skip next 2 dc, (sc, 2 dc) in next dc; repeat from ★ across to last 3 dc, skip next 2 dc, sc in last dc: 81 sts.

Row 3: Ch 3, turn; dc in next st and in each st across to last sc, 2 dc in last sc: 82 dc.

Row 4: Ch 31, turn; (sc, 2 dc) in second ch from hook, ★ skip next 2 sts, (sc, 2 dc) in next st; repeat from ★ across to last 3 dc, skip next 2 dc, sc in last dc: 112 sts.

Row 5: Ch 3, turn; dc in next st and in each st across.

Row 6: Ch 1, turn; (sc, 2 dc) in first dc, ★ skip next 2 dc, (sc, 2 dc) in next dc; repeat from ★ across to last 3 dc, skip next 2 dc, sc in last dc.

Rows 7 thru 13{15-17-19}: Repeat Rows 5 and 6, 3{4-5-6} times; then repeat Row 5 once **more**.

NECK SHAPING

Row 1: Turn; slip st in first 12 sts, ch 1, sc in next 6 dc, hdc in next 6 dc, (sc, 2 dc) in next dc, ★ skip next 2 dc, (sc, 2 dc) in next dc; repeat from ★ across to last 3 dc, skip next 2 dc, sc in last dc: 100 sts.

Row 2: Ch 3, turn; dc in next st and in each st across to last 4 sts, decrease, leave last sc unworked: 97 dc.

Row 3: Turn; slip st in first 9 sts, ch 1, sc in next 6 dc, hdc in next 6 dc, (sc, 2 dc) in next dc, ★ skip next 2 dc, (sc, 2 dc) in next dc; repeat from ★ across to last 3 dc, skip next 2 dc, sc in last dc: 88 sts.

Rows 4-6: Repeat Rows 2 and 3 once, then repeat Row 2 once **more**: 73 dc.

Row 7: Turn; slip st in first 11 sts, ch 1, sc in next 5 dc, hdc in next 6 dc, (sc, 2 dc) in next dc, ★ skip next 2 dc, (sc, 2 dc) in next dc; repeat from ★ across to last 2 dc, skip next dc, sc in last dc: 63 sts.

Row 8: Ch 3, turn; dc in next st and in each st across to last 4 sts, decrease, leave last sc unworked: 60 dc.

Row 9: Turn; slip st in first 5 sts, ch 1, sc in next 5 dc, hdc in next 5 dc, 2 dc in next dc, ★ skip next 2 dc, (sc, 2 dc) in next dc; repeat from ★ across to last 2 dc, skip next dc, sc in last dc; finish off: 55 sts.

Back Panel

The method used to connect the Motifs is a no-sew joining also known as "join-as-you-go." After the First Motif is made, each remaining Motif is worked to the last round, then crocheted together as the last round is worked.

Join Motifs into 3 vertical strips of 6 Motifs each, using One or Two Side Joining. Holding pieces with **wrong** sides together, work a single crochet into space as indicated. When working into a corner space that has been previously joined, work into the joining sc.

FIRST MOTIF

Rnd 1: With larger size hook and Rose, ch 2, 8 sc in second ch from hook; join with slip st to first sc.

Rnd 2: Ch 1, sc in same st, (ch 8, sc in next sc) around, ch 4, tr in first sc to form last ch-8 sp: 8 ch-8 sps.

Rnd 3: Ch 1, sc in last ch-8 sp made, ch 5, sc in same sp, ch 4, sc in next ch-8 sp, ★ ch 4, (sc, ch 5, sc) in next ch-8 sp, ch 4, sc in next ch-8 sp; repeat from ★ around, ch 1, dc in first sc to form last ch-4 sp: 12 sps.

Instructions continued on page 32.

Rnd 4: Ch 1, sc in last ch-4 sp made, work Large Picot, ch 2, sc in next ch-5 sp, work Small Picot 3 times, slip st in last sc made, work Large Picot, ch 2, sc in next ch-4 sp, ch 5, ★ sc in next ch-4 sp, work Large Picot, ch 2, sc in next ch-5 sp, work Small Picot 3 times, slip st in last sc made, work Large Picot, ch 2, sc in next ch-4 sp, ch 5; repeat from ★ 2 times **more**; join with slip st to first sc, finish off.

ADDITIONAL 17 MOTIFS

Work same as First Motif through Rnd 3; do **not** finish off: 12 sps.

ONE SIDE JOINING

Rnd 4 (Joining rnd)**:** Ch 1, sc in last ch-4 sp made, work Large Picot, ch 2, sc in next ch-5 sp, work Small Picot, ch 1; with **right** side of **previous Motif** facing, slip st in center Small Picot on corresponding corner, ch 1, slip st in last ch made on **new Motif,** ch 1, slip st in next Small Picot on **previous Motif,** ch 1, slip st in last sc made on **new Motif,** ch 3, slip st in next Large Picot on **previous Motif,** ch 1, slip st in last ch made on **new Motif,** ch 2, sc in next ch-4 sp, ch 2, slip st in next ch-5 sp on **previous Motif,** ch 2, sc in next ch-4 sp on **new Motif,** ch 3, slip st in next Large Picot on **previous Motif,** ch 1, slip st in last ch made on **new Motif,** ch 2, sc in next ch-5 sp, ch 1, slip st in next Small Picot on **previous Motif,** ch 1, slip st in last ch made on **new Motif,** ch 1, slip st in next Small Picot on **previous Motif,** ch 1, slip st in last ch made on **new Motif,** work Small Picot, slip st in last sc made, work Large Picot, ch 2, sc in next ch-5 sp, ch 5, ★ sc in next ch-4 sp, work Large Picot, ch 2, sc in next ch-5 sp, work Small Picot 3 times, slip st in last sc made, work Large Picot, ch 2, sc in next ch-4 sp, ch 5; repeat from ★ once **more**; join with slip st to first sc, finish off.

TWO SIDE JOINING

Rnd 4 (Joining rnd)**:** Ch 1, sc in last ch-4 sp made, work Large Picot, ch 2, sc in next ch-5 sp, work Small Picot, ch 1; with **right** side of **previous Motif** facing, slip st in center Small Picot on corresponding corner, ch 1, slip st in last ch made on **new Motif,** ★ ch 1, slip st in next Small Picot on **previous Motif,** ch 1, slip st in last sc made on **new Motif,** ch 3, slip st in next Large Picot on **previous Motif,** ch 1, slip st in last ch made on

new Motif, ch 2, sc in next ch-4 sp, ch 2, slip st in next ch-5 sp on **previous Motif,** ch 2, sc in next ch-4 sp on **new Motif,** ch 3, slip st in next Large Picot on **previous Motif,** ch 1, slip st in last ch made on **new Motif,** ch 2, sc in next ch-5 sp, ch 1, slip st in next Small Picot on **previous Motif,** ch 1, slip st in last ch made on **new Motif,** ch 1, slip st in next Small Picot on **previous Motif,** ch 1, slip st in last ch made on **new Motif;** repeat from ★ once **more,** work Small Picot, slip st in last sc made, work Large Picot, ch 2, sc in next ch-4 sp, ch 5, sc in next ch-4 sp, work Large Picot, ch 2, sc in next ch-5 sp, work Small Picot 3 times, slip st in last sc made, work Large Picot, ch 2, sc in next ch-4 sp, ch 5; join with slip st to first sc, finish off.

Finishing

Sew shoulder seams.

Sew center Back Body seam for 5" (12.5 cm) down from neck edge.

With **wrong** sides together and bottom edges of Backs even with short edge of Back Panel, pin Back Panel in place along each edge of Backs.

Left Back Joining: With Back Panel facing, using smaller size hook, working in sts on last row of Left Back **and** in each sp and Picot across Back Panel, join Brown with sc in first st *(see Joining With Sc, page 58)*; sc evenly across; finish off.

Right Back Joining: With Back Panel facing, using smaller size hook, working in free loops of beginning ch on Right Back *(Fig. 3b, page 59)* **and** in each sp and Picot across Back Panel, join Brown with sc in first ch; sc evenly across; finish off.

Pleat the top edge of the Back Panel at the neck edge, placing the center of Back Panel at seam; with **wrong** side facing, sew in place with Brown.

BODY EDGING

With **right** side of Right Back facing and using smaller size hook, join Brown with sc in end of first row; sc evenly spaced around entire piece to last row on Left Back, working 3 sc in each corner and increasing and decreasing as needed for Edging to lay flat; finish off.

ARMHOLE EDGING

With **right** side facing and using smaller size hook, join Brown with sc at bottom of one Armhole; sc evenly spaced around Armhole edge; join with slip st to first sc, finish off.

Repeat around remaining Armhole.

BUTTON TAB (Make 2)

With smaller size hook and Pink, ch 9.

Row 1 (Right side): Sc in second ch from hook and in each ch across: 8 sc.

Note: Mark Row 1 as **right** side.

Row 2: Ch 1, turn; working in Front Loops Only *(Fig. 2, page 58)*, sc in each sc across.

Row 3 (Buttonhole row): Ch 1, turn; working in Front Loops Only, sc in first 3 sc, ch 2, skip next 2 sc, sc in last 3 sc: 6 sc and one ch-2 sp.

Row 4: Ch 1, turn; working in Front Loops Only, sc in first 3 sc, 2 sc in next ch-2 sp, sc in last 3 sc: 8 sc.

Rows 5-9: Ch 1, turn; sc in Front Loops Only of each sc across.

Rows 10-12: Repeat Rows 3-5.

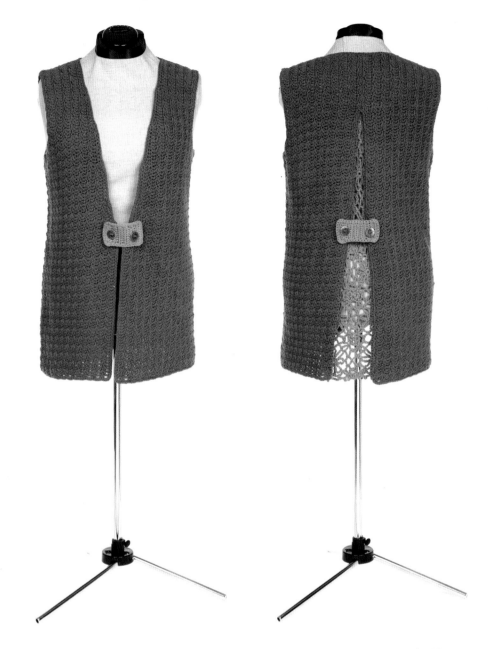

Trim: Ch 1, turn; 3 sc in first sc, sc in next 6 sc, 3 sc in last sc, work 10 sc evenly spaced across end of rows; working in free loops of beginning ch, 3 sc in first ch, sc in next 6 chs, 3 sc in next ch; work 10 sc evenly spaced across end of rows; join with slip st to first sc, finish off.

Using photo as guide for placement, sew buttons to waistline on Fronts and Backs, 1" (2.5 cm) from Front edges and 1" (2.5 cm) from center Back edges.

Button Tabs onto buttons.

Ribbed Waist Tunic

▰▰▱▱ **EASY +**

Size	Finished Chest Measurement
Large	42$^1/_2$" (108 cm)
Extra Large	46" (117 cm)
2X-Large	51$^1/_2$" (131 cm)
3X-Large	57" (145 cm)
4X-Large	62$^1/_2$" (159 cm)

Size Note: Instructions are written with sizes Large and Extra Large in the first set of braces { } and with sizes 2X-Large, 3X-Large, and 4X-Large in the second set of braces. Instructions will be easier to read if you circle all the numbers pertaining to your size. If only one number is given, it applies to all sizes.

MATERIALS

Medium Weight Yarn
[1.76 ounces, 87 yards
(50 grams, 80 meters) per skein]:
  {14-15}{18-21-24} skeins
Crochet hooks, sizes G (4 mm) **and** H (5 mm) **or**
  sizes needed for gauge
Safety pin
Yarn needle
Sewing needle and matching thread
$^7/_8$" (22 mm) Buttons - 10

GAUGES

In Ribbing pattern: With larger size hook,
19 sc and 17 rows = 4" (10 cm) not stretched
In Body pattern: With larger size hook,
one repeat = 2$^3/_4$" (7 cm); 6 rows = 3" (7.5 cm)

Gauge Swatches:

Ribbing (not stretched): 4" (10 cm) square
Work same as Waist Ribbing through Row 17; do **not** finish off.

Body: 8$^1/_2$" x 3" (21.5 cm x 7.5 cm)
With larger size hook, ch 38.
Row 1: Sc in second ch from hook and in each ch across: 37 sc.
Rows 2-6: Work Rows 2-6 of Body: 17 sts and 9 ch–3 sps.
Finish off.

STITCH GUIDE

CLUSTER (uses one sp)
★ YO, insert hook in sp indicated, YO and pull up a loop, YO and draw through 2 loops on hook; repeat from ★ once **more**, YO and draw through all 3 loops on hook.

SINGLE CROCHET DECREASE
  (abbreviated sc decrease) (uses next 2 sts)
Pull up a loop in next 2 sts, YO and draw through all 3 loops on hook **(counts as one sc).**

2-DOUBLE CROCHET DECREASE
  (abbreviated 2-dc decrease) (uses next 2 sts)
★ YO, insert hook in **next** st, YO and pull up a loop, YO and draw through 2 loops on hook; repeat from ★ once **more**, YO and draw through all 3 loops on hook **(counts as one dc).**

3-DOUBLE CROCHET DECREASE
  (abbreviated 3-dc decrease) (uses next 3 sts)
★ YO, insert hook in **next** st, YO and pull up a loop, YO and draw through 2 loops on hook; repeat from ★ 2 times **more**, YO and draw through all 4 loops on hook **(counts as one dc).**

PICOT
Ch 3, sc in top of Cluster just made.

Waist Ribbing

Using larger size hook, ch 20.

Row 1: Sc in back ridge of second ch from hook and each ch across *(Fig. 1, page 58)*: 19 sc.

Rows 2 thru {158-180}{202-224-246}: Ch 1, turn; sc in Back Loop Only of each sc across *(Fig. 2, page 58)*; at the end of the last row, do **not** finish off.

Body

Row 1 (Right side): Ch 1, do **not** turn; working in end of rows, work {181-193}{217-241-265} sc evenly spaced across.

Note: Loop a short piece of yarn around any stitch to mark Row 1 as **right** side.

Row 2: Ch 3 **(counts as first dc, now and throughout)**, turn; dc in next sc, ch 3, skip next 2 sc, sc in next sc, ch 3, skip next 3 sc, sc in next sc, ch 3, ★ skip next 2 sc, dc in next 3 sc, ch 3, skip next 2 sc, sc in next sc, ch 3, skip next 3 sc, sc in next sc, ch 3; repeat from ★ across to last 4 sc, skip next 2 sc, dc in last 2 sc: {46-49}{55-61-67} dc and {45-48}{54-60-66} ch-3 sps.

Instructions continued on page 36.

Row 3: Ch 3, turn; dc in next dc, skip next ch-3 sp, work (Cluster, Picot) 5 times in next ch-3 sp, skip next ch-3 sp, ★ dc in next 3 dc, skip next ch-3 sp, work (Cluster, Picot) 5 times in next ch-3 sp, skip next ch-3 sp; repeat from ★ across to last 2 dc, dc in last 2 dc: {46-49}{55-61-67} dc and {75-80} {90-100-110} Picots.

Row 4: Ch 3, turn; dc in next dc, ch 3, skip next Picot, (sc in next Picot, ch 3, skip next Picot) twice, ★ dc in next 3 dc, ch 3, skip next Picot, (sc in next Picot, ch 3, skip next Picot) twice; repeat from ★ across to last 2 dc, dc in last 2 dc: {46-49}{55-61-67} dc and {45-48} {54-60-66} ch-3 sps.

Rows 5-14: Repeat Rows 3 and 4, 5 times; do **not** finish off.

RIGHT FRONT ARMHOLE AND NECK SHAPING

Row 1: Ch 3, turn; dc in next dc, ★ skip next ch-3 sp, work (Cluster, Picot) 5 times in next ch-3 sp, skip next ch-3 sp, dc in next 3 dc; repeat from ★ {2-2}{3-3-4} times **more**, skip next ch-3 sp, work (Cluster, Picot) in next ch-3 sp, leave remaining sts unworked: {11-11} {14-14-17} dc and {16-16}{21-21-26} Picots.

Row 2: Ch 1, turn; sc in first Picot, ★ dc in next 3 dc, ch 3, skip next Picot, (sc in next Picot, ch 3, skip next Picot) twice; repeat from ★ across to last 2 dc, dc in last 2 dc: {11-11}{14-14-17} dc and {9-9} {12-12-15} ch-3 sps.

Row 3: Ch 3, turn; place marker around dc just made for st placement, dc in next dc, skip next ch-3 sp, work (Cluster, Picot) 4 times in next ch-3 sp, skip next ch-3 sp, ★ dc in next 3 dc, skip next ch-3 sp, work (Cluster, Picot) 5 times in next ch-3 sp, skip next ch-3 sp; repeat from ★ across to last 4 sts, work 3-dc decrease, dc in last sc: {10-10}{13-13-16} dc and {14-14}{19-19-24} Picots.

Row 4: Ch 3, turn; dc in next dc, (ch 3, skip next Picot, sc in next Picot) twice, ★ ch 3, skip next Picot, dc in next 3 dc, (ch 3, skip next Picot, sc in next Picot) twice; repeat from ★ across to last 2 dc, dc in last 2 dc: {10-10} {13-13-16} dc and {8-8}{11-11-14} ch-3 sps.

Row 5: Ch 3, turn; dc in next dc, work (Cluster, Picot) twice in next ch-3 sp, skip next ch-3 sp, ★ dc in next 3 dc, skip next ch-3 sp, work (Cluster, Picot) 5 times in next ch-3 sp, skip next ch-3 sp; repeat from ★ across to last 2 dc, dc in last 2 dc: {10-10}{13-13-16} dc and {12-12}{17-17-22} Picots.

Row 6: Ch 3, turn; dc in next dc, ★ ch 3, skip next Picot, (sc in next Picot, ch 3, skip next Picot) twice, dc in next 3 dc; repeat from ★ across to last 2 Picots, ch 3, skip next Picot, sc in next Picot, dc in last 2 dc: {10-10} {13-13-16} dc and {7-7}{10-10-13} ch-3 sps.

Row 7: Ch 3, turn; dc in next dc, skip next ch-3 sp, ★ dc in next 3 dc, skip next ch-3 sp, work (Cluster, Picot) 5 times in next ch-3 sp, skip next ch-3 sp; repeat from ★ {1-1}{1-1-2} time(s) **more**, dc in last 2 dc: {10-10}{13-13-16} dc and {10-10}{15-15-20} Picots.

Row 8: Ch 3, turn; dc in next dc, ch 3, skip next Picot, (sc in next Picot, ch 3, skip next Picot) twice, ★ dc in next 3 dc, ch 3, skip next Picot, (sc in next Picot, ch 3, skip next Picot) twice; repeat from ★ {0-0}{2-2-3} time(s) **more** *(see Zeros, page 58)*, dc in last 5 dc: {10-10}{13-13-16} dc and {6-6}{9-9-12} ch-3 sps.

Row 9: Ch 3, turn; work 2-dc decrease, dc in next 2 dc, skip next ch-3 sp, work (Cluster, Picot) 5 times in next ch-3 sp, skip next ch-3 sp, ★ dc in next 3 dc, skip next ch-3 sp, work (Cluster, Picot) 5 times in next ch-3 sp, skip next ch-3 sp; repeat from ★ {0-0}{1-1-2} time(s) **more**, dc in last 2 dc: {9-9}{12-12-15} dc and {10-10} {15-15-20} Picots.

Row 10: Ch 3, turn; dc in next dc, ch 3, skip next Picot, (sc in next Picot, ch 3, skip next Picot) twice, ★ dc in next 3 dc, ch 3, skip next Picot, (sc in next Picot, ch 3, skip next Picot) twice; repeat from ★ {0-0}{1-1-2} time(s) **more**, dc in last 4 dc: {9-9}{12-12-15} dc and {6-6}{9-9-12} ch-3 sps.

Row 11: Ch 3, turn; work 2-dc decrease, dc in next dc, skip next ch-3 sp, work (Cluster, Picot) 5 times in next ch-3 sp, skip next ch-3 sp, ★ dc in next 3 dc, skip next ch-3 sp, work (Cluster, Picot) 5 times in next ch-3 sp, skip next ch-3 sp; repeat from ★ {0-0}{1-1-2} time(s) **more**, dc in last 2 dc: {8-8}{11-11-14} dc and {10-10} {15-15-20} Picots.

Row 12: Ch 3, turn; dc in next dc, ch 3, skip next Picot, (sc in next Picot, ch 3, skip next Picot) twice, ★ dc in next 3 dc, ch 3, skip next Picot, (sc in next Picot, ch 3, skip next Picot) twice; repeat from ★ {0-0}{1-1-2} time(s) **more**, dc in last 3 dc: {8-8}{11-11-14} dc and {6-6}{9-9-12} ch-3 sps.

Row 13: Ch 3, turn; work 2-dc decrease, skip next ch-3 sp, work (Cluster, Picot) 5 times in next ch-3 sp, skip next ch-3 sp, ★ dc in next 3 dc, skip next ch-3 sp, work (Cluster, Picot) 5 times in next ch-3 sp, skip next ch-3 sp; repeat from ★ {0-0}{1-1-2} time(s) **more**, dc in last 2 dc: {7-7}{10-10-13} dc and {10-10} {15-15-20} Picots.

Size Extra Large Only

Row 14: Ch 3, turn; dc in next dc, ch 3, skip next Picot, (sc in next Picot, ch 3, skip next Picot) twice, dc in next 3 dc, ch 3, skip next Picot, (sc in next Picot, ch 3, skip next Picot) twice, dc in last 2 dc: 7 dc and 6 ch-3 sps.

Row 15: Ch 3, turn; dc in next dc, skip next ch-3 sp, work (Cluster, Picot) 5 times in next ch-3 sp, skip next ch-3 sp, dc in next 3 dc, skip next ch-3 sp, work (Cluster, Picot) 5 times in next ch-3 sp, skip next ch-3 sp, dc in last 2 dc: 7 dc and 10 Picots.

Repeat Rows 14 and 15 until Armholes measure approximately 8" (20.5 cm).

Finish off.

Instructions continued on page 38.

All Other Sizes

Row 14: Ch 3, turn; dc in next dc, ch 3, skip next Picot, (sc in next Picot, ch 3, skip next Picot) twice, ★ dc in next 3 dc, ch 3, skip next Picot, (sc in next Picot, ch 3, skip next Picot) twice; repeat from ★ once **more**, dc in last 2 dc: {10}{10-10-13} dc and {9}{9-9-12} ch-3 sps.

Row 15: Ch 3, turn; dc in next dc, skip next ch-3 sp, work (Cluster, Picot) 3 times in next ch-3 sp, skip next ch-3 sp, ★ dc in next 3 dc, skip next ch-3 sp, work (Cluster, Picot) 5 times in next ch-3 sp, skip next ch-3 sp; repeat from ★ once **more**, dc in last 2 dc: {10}{10-13-13} dc and {13}{13-13-18} Picots.

Row 16: Ch 3, turn; dc in next dc, (ch 3, skip next Picot, sc in next Picot) twice, ★ ch 3, skip next Picot, dc in next 3 dc, (ch 3, skip next Picot, sc in next Picot) twice; repeat from ★ once **more**, dc in last 2 dc: {10}{10-13-13} dc and {8}{8-8-11} ch-3 sps.

Row 17: Ch 3, turn; dc in next dc, work (Cluster, Picot) 3 times in next ch-3 sp, skip next ch-3 sp, ★ dc in next 3 dc, skip next ch-3 sp, work (Cluster, Picot) 5 times in next ch-3 sp, skip next ch-3 sp; repeat from ★ once **more**, dc in last 2 dc.

Row 18: Ch 3, turn; dc in next dc, ch 3, skip next Picot, (sc in next Picot, ch 3, skip next Picot) twice, ★ dc in next 3 dc, ch 3, skip next Picot, (sc in next Picot, ch 3, skip next Picot) twice; repeat from ★ once **more**, dc in last 2 dc.

Repeat Rows 17 and 18 until Armholes measure approximately {7}{9-10³/₄}"/{18}{23-27.5} cm.

Finish off.

BACK ARMHOLE SHAPING

Row 1: With **right** side facing, skip next 2 ch-3 sps from Right Front and join yarn with dc in next ch-3 sp *(see Joining With Dc, page 58)*; work (Cluster, Picot) in same sp, skip next ch-3 sp, dc in next 3 dc, skip next ch-3 sp, ★ work (Cluster, Picot) 5 times in next ch-3 sp, skip next ch-3 sp, dc in next 3 dc, skip next ch-3 sp; repeat from ★ {3-5}{5-7-7} times **more**, work (Cluster, Picot) in next ch-3 sp, leave remaining sts unworked: {16-22}{22-28-28} dc and {22-32}{32-42-42} Picots.

Row 2: Ch 1, turn; sc in first Picot, work 2-dc decrease, dc in next dc, ch 3, skip next Picot, (sc in next Picot, ch 3, skip next Picot) twice, ★ dc in next 3 dc, ch 3, skip next Picot, (sc in next Picot, ch 3, skip next Picot) twice; repeat from ★ across to last 5 sts, dc in next dc, work 2-dc decrease, skip next Picot, dc in last dc: {14-20}{20-26-26} dc and {12-18}{18-24-24} ch-3 sps.

Row 3: Ch 3, turn; skip next dc, dc in next dc, skip next ch-3 sp, work (Cluster, Picot) 5 times in next ch-3 sp, skip next ch-3 sp, ★ dc in next 3 dc, skip next ch-3 sp, work (Cluster, Picot) 5 times in next ch-3 sp, skip next ch-3 sp; repeat from ★ across to last 3 sts, dc in next dc, skip next dc, dc in last sc: {13-19}{19-25-25} dc and {20-30}{30-40-40} Picots.

Row 4: Ch 3, turn; dc in next dc, ch 3, skip next Picot, (sc in next Picot, ch 3, skip next Picot) twice, ★ dc in next 3 dc, ch 3, skip next Picot, (sc in next Picot, ch 3, skip next Picot) twice; repeat from ★ across to last 2 dc, dc in last 2 dc: {13-19}{19-25-25} dc and {12-18}{18-24-24} ch-3 sps.

Row 5: Ch 3, turn; dc in next dc, skip next ch-3 sp, work (Cluster, Picot) 5 times in next ch-3 sp, skip next ch-3 sp, ★ dc in next 3 dc, skip next ch-3 sp, work (Cluster, Picot) 5 times in next ch-3 sp, skip next ch-3 sp; repeat from ★ across to last 2 dc, dc in last 2 dc: {13-19}{19-25-25} dc and {20-30}{30-40-40} Picots.

Repeat Rows 4 and 5 until Back measures same as Right Front.

Finish off.

LEFT FRONT ARMHOLE AND NECK SHAPING

Row 1: With **right** side facing, skip next 2 ch-3 sps from Back and join yarn with dc in next ch-3 sp; work (Cluster, Picot) in same sp, skip next ch-3 sp, ★ dc in next 3 dc, skip next ch-3 sp, work (Cluster, Picot) 5 times in next ch-3 sp, skip next ch-3 sp; repeat from ★ across to last 2 dc, dc in last 2 dc: {12-12}{15-15-18} dc and {16-16}{21-21-26} Picots.

Row 2: Ch 3, turn; dc in next dc, ★ ch 3, skip next Picot, (sc in next Picot, ch 3, skip next Picot) twice, dc in next 3 dc; repeat from ★ across to last Picot, sc in last Picot, leave last dc unworked: {11-11}{14-14-17} dc and {9-9}{12-12-15} ch-3 sps.

Row 3: Ch 3, turn; work 3-dc decrease, ★ skip next ch-3 sp, work (Cluster, Picot) 5 times in next ch-3 sp, skip next ch-3 sp, dc in next 3 dc; repeat from ★ across to last 3 ch-3 sps, skip next ch-3 sp, work (Cluster, Picot) 4 times in next ch-3 sp, skip next ch-3 sp, dc in last 2 dc, place marker around last dc made for st placement: {10-10}{13-13-16} dc and {14-14}{19-19-24} Picots.

Row 4: Ch 3, turn; dc in next dc, (sc in next Picot, ch 3, skip next Picot) twice, ★ dc in next 3 dc, ch 3, skip next Picot, (sc in next Picot, ch 3, skip next Picot) twice; repeat from ★ across to last 2 dc, dc in last 2 dc: {10-10}{13-13-16} dc and {8-8}{11-11-14} ch-3 sps.

Row 5: Ch 3, turn; dc in next dc, ★ skip next ch-3 sp, work (Cluster, Picot) 5 times in next ch-3 sp, skip next ch-3 sp, dc in next 3 dc; repeat from ★ across to last 2 ch-3 sps, skip next ch-3 sp, work (Cluster, Picot) twice in next ch-3 sp, dc in last 2 dc: {10-10}{13-13-16} dc and {12-12}{17-17-22} Picots.

Row 6: Ch 3, turn; dc in next dc, sc in next Picot, ch 3, skip next Picot, ★ dc in next 3 dc, ch 3, skip next Picot, (sc in next Picot, ch 3, skip next Picot) twice; repeat from ★ across to last 2 dc, dc in last 2 dc: {10-10}{13-13-16} dc and {7-7}{10-10-13} ch-3 sps.

Row 7: Ch 3, turn; dc in next dc, skip next ch-3 sp, ★ work (Cluster, Picot) 5 times in next ch-3 sp, skip next ch-3 sp, dc in next 3 dc, skip next ch-3 sp; repeat from ★ {1-1}{1-1-2} time(s) **more**, dc in last 2 dc: {10-10}{13-13-16} dc and {10-10}{15-15-20} Picots.

Row 8: Ch 3, turn; dc in next 4 dc, ch 3, skip next Picot, (sc in next Picot, ch 3, skip next Picot) twice, ★ dc in next 3 dc, ch 3, skip next Picot, (sc in next Picot, ch 3, skip next Picot) twice; repeat from ★ {0-0}{1-1-2} time(s) **more**, dc in last 2 dc: {10-10}{13-13-16} dc and {6-6}{9-9-12} ch-3 sps.

Row 9: Ch 3, turn; dc in next dc, skip next ch-3 sp, work (Cluster, Picot) 5 times in next ch-3 sp, skip next ch-3 sp, ★ dc in next 3 dc, skip next ch-3 sp, work (Cluster, Picot) 5 times in next ch-3 sp, skip next ch-3 sp; repeat from ★ {0-0}{2-2-3} time(s) **more**, dc in next 2 dc, work 2-dc decrease, dc in last dc: {9-9}{12-12-15} dc and {10-10}{15-15-20} Picots.

Row 10: Ch 3, turn; dc in next 3 dc, ch 3, skip next Picot, (sc in next Picot, ch 3, skip next Picot) twice, ★ dc in next 3 dc, ch 3, skip next Picot, (sc in next Picot, ch 3, skip next Picot) twice; repeat from ★ {0-0}{1-1-2} time(s) **more**, dc in last 2 dc: {9-9}{12-12-15} dc and {6-6}{9-9-12} ch-3 sps.

Row 11: Ch 3, turn; dc in next dc, skip next ch-3 sp, work (Cluster, Picot) 5 times in next ch-3 sp, skip next ch-3 sp, ★ dc in next 3 dc, skip next ch-3 sp, work (Cluster, Picot) 5 times in next ch-3 sp, skip next ch-3 sp; repeat from ★ {0-0}{1-1-2} time(s) **more**, dc in next dc, work 2-dc decrease, dc in last dc: {8-8}{11-11-14} dc and {10-10}{15-15-20} Picots.

Instructions continued on page 40.

Row 12: Ch 3, turn; dc in next 2 dc, (ch 3, skip next Picot, sc in next Picot) twice, ch 3, skip next Picot, ★ dc in next 3 dc, (ch 3, skip next Picot, sc in next Picot) twice, ch 3, skip next Picot; repeat from ★ {0-0}{1-1-2} time(s) **more**, dc in last 2 dc: {8-8}{11-11-14} dc and {6-6}{9-9-12} ch-3 sps.

Row 13: Ch 3, turn; dc in next dc, skip next ch-3 sp, work (Cluster, Picot) 5 times in next ch-3 sp, skip next ch-3 sp, ★ dc in next 3 dc, skip next ch-3 sp, work (Cluster, Picot) 5 times in next ch-3 sp, skip next ch-3 sp; repeat from ★ {0-0}{1-1-2} time(s) **more**, work 2-dc decrease, dc in last dc: {7-7}{10-10-13} dc and {10-10}{15-15-20} Picots.

Size Large Only
Work same as Right Front.

All Other Sizes
Work same as Right Front.

Skirt

Row 1 (Right side): With **right** side facing and working in end of rows along opposite edge of Waist Ribbing, join yarn with sc in first row *(see Joining With Sc, page 58)*; work {168-192}{216-240-264} sc evenly spaced across: {181-193}{217-241-265} sc.

Row 2: Ch 3, turn; dc in next sc, ch 3, skip next 2 sc, sc in next sc, ch 3, skip next 3 sc, sc in next sc, ch 3, ★ skip next 2 sc, dc in next 3 sc, ch 3, skip next 2 sc, sc in next sc, ch 3, skip next 3 sc, sc in next sc, ch 3; repeat from ★ across to last 4 sc, skip next 2 sc, dc in last 2 sc: {46-49} {55-61-67} dc and {45-48}{54-60-66} ch-3 sps.

Row 3: Ch 3, turn; dc in next dc, skip next ch-3 sp, work (Cluster, Picot) 5 times in next ch-3 sp, skip next ch-3 sp, † dc in next 3 dc, skip next ch-3 sp, work (Cluster, Picot) 5 times in next ch-3 sp, skip next ch-3 sp †; repeat from † to † {2-2}{2-4-4} times **more**, ♥ dc in next dc, 2 dc in next dc, dc in next dc, skip next ch-3 sp, work (Cluster, Picot) 5 times in next ch-3 sp, skip next ch-3 sp ♥, repeat from † to † {0-1}{2-0-1} time(s), repeat from ♥ to ♥ once, repeat from † to † {3-3}{3-5-5} times, repeat from ♥ to ♥ once, repeat from † to † {0-1}{2-0-1} time(s), repeat from ♥ to ♥ once, repeat from † to † across to last 2 dc, dc in last 2 dc: {50-53}{59-65-71} dc and {70-80}{90-100-110} Picots.

Row 4: Ch 3, turn; dc in next dc, ch 3, skip next Picot, (sc in next Picot, ch 3, skip next Picot) twice, † dc in next 3 dc, ch 3, skip next Picot, (sc in next Picot, ch 3, skip next Picot) twice †; repeat from † to † {2-2} {2-4-4} times **more**, ♥ dc in next 4 dc, ch 3, skip next Picot, (sc in next Picot, ch 3, skip next Picot) twice ♥, repeat from † to † {0-1}{2-0-1} time(s), repeat from ♥ to ♥ once, repeat from † to † {3-3}{3-5-5} times, repeat from ♥ to ♥ once, repeat from † to † {0-1} {2-0-1} time(s), repeat from ♥ to ♥ once, repeat from † to † across to last 2 dc, dc in last 2 dc: {50-53} {59-65-71} dc and {42-48}{54-60-66} ch-3 sps.

Row 5: Ch 3, turn; dc in next dc, skip next ch-3 sp, work (Cluster, Picot) 5 times in next ch-3 sp, skip next ch-3 sp, † dc in next 3 dc, skip next ch-3 sp, work (Cluster, Picot) 5 times in next ch-3 sp, skip next ch-3 sp †; repeat from † to † {2-2}{2-4-4} times **more**, ♥ dc in next 2 dc, dc in sp **before** next dc *(Fig. 5, page 59)*, dc in next 2 dc, skip next ch-3 sp, work (Cluster, Picot) 5 times in next ch-3 sp, skip next ch-3 sp ♥, repeat from † to † {0-1}{2-0-1} time(s), repeat from ♥ to ♥ once, repeat from † to † {3-3}{3-5-5} times, repeat from ♥ to ♥ once, repeat from † to † {0-1}{2-0-1} time(s), repeat from ♥ to ♥ once, repeat from † to † across to last 2 dc, dc in last 2 dc: {54-57}{63-69-75} dc and {70-80} {90-100-110} Picots.

Row 6: Ch 3, turn; dc in next dc, ch 3, skip next Picot, (sc in next Picot, ch 3, skip next Picot) twice, † dc in next 3 dc, ch 3, skip next Picot, (sc in next Picot, ch 3, skip next Picot) twice †; repeat from † to † {2-2} {2-4-4} times **more**, ♥ dc in next 5 dc, ch 3, skip next Picot, (sc in next Picot, ch 3, skip next Picot) twice ♥, repeat from † to † {0-1}{2-0-1} time(s), repeat from ♥ to ♥ once, repeat from † to † {3-3}{3-5-5} times, repeat from ♥ to ♥ once, repeat from † to † {0-1} {2-0-1} time(s), repeat from ♥ to ♥ once, repeat from † to † across to last 2 dc, dc in last 2 dc: {54-57} {63-69-75} dc and {42-48}{54-60-66} ch-3 sps.

Row 7: Ch 3, turn; dc in next dc, skip next ch-3 sp, work (Cluster, Picot) 5 times in next ch-3 sp, skip next ch-3 sp, † dc in next 3 dc, skip next ch-3 sp, work (Cluster, Picot) 5 times in next ch-3 sp, skip next ch-3 sp †; repeat from † to † {2-2}{2-4-4} times **more**, ♥ dc in next 2 dc, 2 dc in next dc, dc in next 2 dc, skip next ch-3 sp, work (Cluster, Picot) 5 times in next ch-3 sp, skip next ch-3 sp ♥, repeat from † to † {0-1} {2-0-1} time(s), repeat from ♥ to ♥ once, repeat from † to † {3-3}{3-5-5} times, repeat from ♥ to ♥ once, repeat from † to † {0-1}{2-0-1} time(s), repeat from ♥ to ♥ once, repeat from † to † across to last 2 dc, dc in last 2 dc: {58-61}{67-73-79} dc and {70-80} {90-100-110} Picots.

Row 8: Ch 3, turn; dc in next dc, ch 3, skip next Picot, (sc in next Picot, ch 3, skip next Picot) twice, † dc in next 3 dc, ch 3, skip next Picot, (sc in next Picot, ch 3, skip next Picot) twice †; repeat from † to † {2-2} {2-4-4} times **more**, ♥ dc in next 6 dc, ch 3, skip next Picot, (sc in next Picot, ch 3, skip next Picot) twice ♥, repeat from † to † {0-1}{2-0-1} time(s), repeat from ♥ to ♥ once, repeat from † to † {3-3}{3-5-5} times, repeat from ♥ to ♥ once, repeat from † to † {0-1} {2-0-1} time(s), repeat from ♥ to ♥ once, repeat from † to † across to last 2 dc, dc in last 2 dc: {58-61} {67-73-79} dc and {42-48}{54-60-66} ch-3 sps.

Row 9: Ch 3, turn; dc in next dc, skip next ch-3 sp, work (Cluster, Picot) 5 times in next ch-3 sp, skip next ch-3 sp, † dc in next 3 dc, skip next ch-3 sp, work (Cluster, Picot) 5 times in next ch-3 sp, skip next ch-3 sp †; repeat from † to † {2-2}{2-4-4} times **more**, ♥ dc in next 3 dc, dc in sp **before** next dc, dc in next 3 dc, skip next ch-3 sp, work (Cluster, Picot) 5 times in next ch-3 sp, skip next ch-3 sp ♥, repeat from † to † {0-1}{2-0-1} time(s), repeat from ♥ to ♥ once, repeat from † to † {3-3}{3-5-5} times, repeat from ♥ to ♥ once, repeat from † to † {0-1}{2-0-1} time(s), repeat from ♥ to ♥ once, repeat from † to † across to last 2 dc, dc in last 2 dc: {62-65}{71-77-83} dc and {70-80} {90-100-110} Picots.

Row 10: Ch 3, turn; dc in next dc, ch 3, skip next Picot, (sc in next Picot, ch 3, skip next Picot) twice, † dc in next 3 dc, ch 3, skip next Picot, (sc in next Picot, ch 3, skip next Picot) twice †; repeat from † to † {2-2} {2-4-4} times **more**, ♥ dc in next 7 dc, ch 3, skip next Picot, (sc in next Picot, ch 3, skip next Picot) twice ♥, repeat from † to † {0-1}{2-0-1} time(s), repeat from ♥ to ♥ once, repeat from † to † {3-3}{3-5-5} times, repeat from ♥ to ♥ once, repeat from † to † {0-1} {2-0-1} time(s), repeat from ♥ to ♥ once, repeat from † to † across to last 2 dc, dc in last 2 dc: {62-65} {71-77-83} dc and {42-48}{54-60-66} ch-3 sps.

Instructions continued on page 42.

Row 11: Ch 3, turn; dc in next dc, skip next ch-3 sp, work (Cluster, Picot) 5 times in next ch-3 sp, skip next ch-3 sp, † dc in next 3 dc, skip next ch-3 sp, work (Cluster, Picot) 5 times in next ch-3 sp, skip next ch-3 sp †; repeat from † to † {2-2}{2-4-4} times **more**, ♥ dc in next 7 dc, skip next ch-3 sp, work (Cluster, Picot) 5 times in next ch-3 sp, skip next ch-3 sp ♥, repeat from † to † {0-1}{2-0-1} time(s), repeat from ♥ to ♥ once, repeat from † to † {3-3}{3-5-5} times, repeat from ♥ to ♥ once, repeat from † to † {0-1} {2-0-1} time(s), repeat from ♥ to ♥ once, repeat from † to † across to last 2 dc, dc in last 2 dc: {68-65} {71-77-83} dc and {70-80}{90-100-110} Picots.

Rows 12-19: Repeat Rows 10 and 11, 4 times.

Do **not** finish off, place loop onto safety pin to keep piece from unraveling as you sew shoulder seams.

Finishing

Sew shoulder seams.

FRONT BAND

Row 1: Slip loop from safety pin onto smaller size hook, with **right** side facing and working in end of rows; ch 1, work 102 sc evenly spaced across Right Front edge to marked row, 4 sc in marked row, work {32-32}{36-36-40} sc evenly spaced across Right Neck Shaping, place marker around last sc made for st placement, work {23-23}{34-34-40} sc evenly spaced across Back neck, place marker around last sc made for st placement, work {32-32}{36-36-40} sc evenly spaced across left neck edge to marked row, 4 sc in marked row, work 102 sc evenly spaced across Left Front edge: {299-299}{318-318-332} sc.

Rows 2-4: Ch 1, turn; sc decrease, (sc in each sc across to next marked sc, sc decrease, remove marker and place around last sc made) twice, sc in each sc across to last 2 sc, sc decrease; at end of Row 4, remove markers: {283-283}{302-302-316} sc.

Row 5 (Buttonhole row)**:** Ch 1, turn; sc decrease, sc in next 39 sc, ch 2, skip next 2 sc, ★ sc in next 12 sc, ch 2, skip next 2 sc; repeat from ★ 3 times **more**, sc in each sc across to last 2 sc, sc decrease: {271-271} {290-290-304} and 5 ch-2 sps.

Row 6: Ch 1, turn; sc decrease, ★ sc in each sc across to next ch-2 sp, 2 sc in next ch-2 sp; repeat from ★ 4 times **more**, sc in each sc across to last 2 sc, sc decrease: {279-279}{298-298-312} sc.

Rows 7 and 8: Ch 1, turn; sc decrease, sc in each sc across to last 2 sc, sc decrease: {275-275}{294-294-308} sc.

Finish off.

ARMHOLE BAND

Rnd 1: With **right** side facing and smaller size hook, join yarn with sc in center st of armhole; work {78-96}{100-120-130} sc evenly spaced around armhole edge; join with slip st to first sc: {79-97}{101-121-131} sc.

Rnds 2-5: Ch 1, turn; sc decrease, sc in each sc around to last 2 sc, sc decrease; join with slip st to first sc.

Finish off.

Repeat around second Armhole.

Sew first 5 buttons to Left Front Band opposite buttonholes.

Sew next 3 buttons to Left Front Band evenly spaced above top button.

Sew remaining 2 buttons to Left Front Band evenly spaced below bottom button.

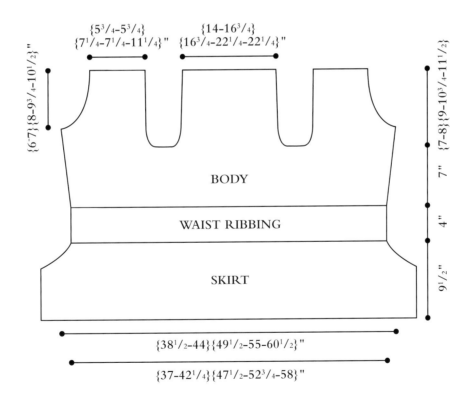

Tie Back Tunic

Size	Finished Chest Measurement	
Large	44"	(112 cm)
Extra Large	48"	(122 cm)
2X-Large	52"	(132 cm)
3X-Large	56"	(142 cm)
4X-Large	60"	(152.5 cm)

Size Note: Instructions are written with sizes Large and Extra Large in the first set of braces { } and with sizes 2X-Large, 3X-Large, and 4X-Large in the second set of braces. Instructions will be easier to read if you circle all the numbers pertaining to your size. If only one number is given, it applies to all sizes.

MATERIALS

SUPER FINE **1**

Super Fine Weight Yarn
[3.5 ounces, 433 yards
(100 grams, 400 meters) per hank]:
  Maroon - {6-6}{7-8-9} hanks
  Rust - {1-1}{2-2-2} hank(s)
Crochet hook, size F (3.75 mm) **or** size needed
  for gauge
Yarn needle

GAUGE: In pattern, 2 repeats = 3³/₄" (9.5 cm);
        16 rows = 4" (10 cm)

Gauge Swatch: 3³/₄" x 4" (9.5 cm x 10 cm)
Ch 30.
Work same as Body for 16 rows.
Finish off.

Back

BODY
With Maroon, ch {186-198}{210-222-234}.

Row 1 (Right side): Dc in sixth ch from hook **(5 skipped chs count as first dc plus ch 2)**, skip next 3 chs, sc in next 5 chs, ★ skip next 3 chs, dc in next ch, (ch 2, dc in same st) twice, skip next 3 chs, sc in next 5 chs; repeat from ★ across to last 4 chs, skip next 3 chs, (dc, ch 2, dc) in last ch: {121-129}{137-145-153} sts and {30-32}{34-36-38} ch-2 sps.

Note: Loop a short piece of yarn around any stitch to mark Row 1 as **right** side.

Row 2: Ch 3 **(counts as first dc, now and throughout)**, turn; 4 dc in next ch-2 sp, skip next 2 sts, sc in next 3 sc, ★ skip next 2 sts, 4 dc in next ch-2 sp, dc in next dc, 4 dc in next ch-2 sp, skip next 2 sts, sc in next 3 sc; repeat from ★ across to last 3 sts, skip next 2 sts, 4 dc in last ch-2 sp, dc in last dc: {181-193}{205-217-229} sts.

Row 3: Ch 1, turn; sc in first 3 dc, skip next 3 sts, dc in next sc, (ch 2, dc in same st) twice, ★ skip next 3 sts, sc in next 5 dc, skip next 3 sts, dc in next sc, (ch 2, dc in same st) twice; repeat from ★ across to last 6 sts, skip next 3 sts, sc in last 3 dc: {121-129}{137-145-153} sts and {30-32}{34-36-38} ch-2 sps.

Row 4: Ch 1, turn; sc in first 2 sc, skip next 2 sts, 4 dc in next ch-2 sp, dc in next dc, 4 dc in next ch-2 sp, ★ skip next 2 sts, sc in next 3 sc, skip next 2 sts, 4 dc in next ch-2 sp, dc in next dc, 4 dc in next ch-2 sp; repeat from ★ across to last 4 sts, skip next 2 sts, sc in last 2 sc: {181-193}{205-217-229} sts.

Row 5: Ch 5 (counts as first dc plus ch 2, now and throughout), turn; dc in same st, skip next 3 sts, sc in next 5 dc, ★ skip next 3 sts, dc in next sc, (ch 2, dc in same st) twice, skip next 3 sts, sc in next 5 dc; repeat from ★ across to last 4 sts, skip next 3 sts, (dc, ch 2, dc) in last sc: {121-129}{137-145-153} sts and {30-32}{34-36-38} ch-2 sps.

Rows 6-30: Repeat Rows 2-5, 6 times; then repeat Row 2 once **more**: {181-193}{205-217-229} sts.

Row 31: Ch 1, turn; sc in first 3 dc, skip next 3 sts, (dc, ch 2, dc) in next sc, skip next 3 sts, sc in next 5 dc, ★ skip next 3 sts, dc in next sc, (ch 2, dc in same st) twice, skip next 3 sts, sc in next 5 dc; repeat from ★ across to last 10 sts, skip next 3 sts, (dc, ch 2, dc) in next sc, skip next 3 sts, sc in last 3 dc: {119-127}{135-143-151} sts and {28-30}{32-34-36} ch-2 sps.

Row 32: Ch 1, turn; sc in first 2 sc, skip next 2 sts, 5 dc in next ch-2 sp, skip next 2 sts, sc in next 3 sc, ★ skip next 2 sts, 4 dc in next ch-2 sp, dc in next dc, 4 dc in next ch-2 sp, skip next 2 sts, sc in next 3 sc; repeat from ★ across to last 6 sts, skip next 2 sts, 5 dc in last ch-2 sp, skip next 2 sts, sc in last 2 sc: {173-185}{197-209-221} sts.

Instructions continued on page 46.

Row 33: Ch 5, turn; dc in same st, skip next 2 sts, sc in next 3 dc, skip next 2 sts, dc in next sc, (ch 2, dc in same st) twice, ★ skip next 3 sts, sc in next 5 dc, skip next 3 sts, dc in next sc, (ch 2, dc in same st) twice; repeat from ★ across to last 8 sts, skip next 2 sts, sc in next 3 dc, skip next 2 sts, (dc, ch 2, dc) in last sc: {117-125}{133-141-149} sts and {30-32}{34-36-38} ch-2 sps.

Row 34: Ch 3, turn; 4 dc in next ch-2 sp, skip next 2 sts, sc in next sc, skip next 2 sts, 4 dc in next ch-2 sp, dc in next dc, 4 dc in next ch-2 sp, ★ skip next 2 sts, sc in next 3 sc, skip next 2 sts, 4 dc in next ch-2 sp, dc in next dc, 4 dc in next ch-2 sp; repeat from ★ across to last 6 sts, skip next 2 sts, sc in next sc, skip next 2 sts, 4 dc in last ch-2 sp, dc in last dc: {177-189}{201-213-225} sts.

Row 35: Ch 1, turn; sc in first 3 dc, skip next 2 dc, (dc, ch 2, dc) in next sc, skip next 2 dc, sc in next 5 dc, ★ skip next 3 sts, dc in next sc, (ch 2, dc in same st) twice, skip next 3 sts, sc in next 5 dc; repeat from ★ across to last 8 sts, skip next 2 dc, (dc, ch 2, dc) in next sc, skip next 2 dc, sc in last 3 dc: {119-127}{135-143-151} sts and {28-30}{32-34-36} ch-2 sps.

Rows 36-44: Repeat Rows 32-35 twice; then repeat Row 32 once **more**: {173-185}{197-209-221} sts.

Row 45: Ch 5, turn; dc in same st, skip next 2 sts, sc in next 3 dc, skip next 2 sts, (dc, ch 2, dc) in next sc, skip next 3 sts, sc in next 5 dc, ★ skip next 3 sts, dc in next sc, (ch 2, dc in same st) twice, skip next 3 sts, sc in next 5 dc; repeat from ★ across to last 12 sts, skip next 3 sts, (dc, ch 2, dc) in next sc, skip next 2 sts, sc in next 3 dc, skip next 2 sts, (dc, ch 2, dc) in last sc: {115-123}{131-139-147} sts and {28-30}{32-34-36} ch-2 sps.

Row 46: Ch 3, turn; 4 dc in next ch-2 sp, skip next 2 sts, sc in next sc, skip next 2 sts, 5 dc in next ch-2 sp, skip next 2 sts, sc in next 3 sc, ★ skip next 2 sts, 4 dc in next ch-2 sp, dc in next dc, 4 dc in next ch-2 sp, skip next 2 sts, sc in next 3 sc; repeat from ★ across to last 8 sts, skip next 2 sts, 5 dc in next ch-2 sp, skip next 2 sts, sc in next sc, skip next 2 sts, 4 dc in next ch-2 sp, dc in last dc: {169-181}{193-205-217} sts.

Row 47: Ch 1, turn; sc in first 3 dc, skip next 2 dc, (dc, ch 2, dc) in next sc, skip next dc, sc in next 3 dc, skip next 2 sts, dc in next sc, (ch 2, dc in same st) twice, ★ skip next 3 sts, sc in next 5 dc, skip next 3 sts, dc in next sc, (ch 2, dc in same st) twice; repeat from ★ across to last 12 sts, skip next 2 sts, sc in next 3 dc, skip next dc, (dc, ch 2, dc) in next sc, skip next 2 dc, sc in last 3 dc: {115-123}{131-139-147} sts and {28-30}{32-34-36} ch-2 sps.

Row 48: Ch 1, turn; sc in first 2 sc, skip next 2 sts, 5 dc in next ch-2 sp, skip next 2 sts, sc in next sc, skip next 2 sts, 4 dc in next ch-2 sp, dc in next dc, 4 dc in next ch-2 sp, ★ skip next 2 sts, sc in next 3 sc, skip next 2 sts, 4 dc in next ch-2 sp, dc in next dc, 4 dc in next ch-2 sp; repeat from ★ across to last 9 sts, skip next 2 sts, sc in next sc, skip next 2 sts, 5 dc in next ch-2 sp, skip next 2 sts, sc in last 2 sc: {169-181}{193-205-217} sts.

Row 49: Ch 5, turn; dc in same st, skip next 2 sts, sc in next 3 dc, skip next dc, (dc, ch 2, dc) in next sc, skip next 2 dc, sc in next 5 dc, ★ skip next 3 sts, dc in next sc, (ch 2, dc in same st) twice, skip next 3 sts, sc in next 5 dc; repeat from ★ across to last 10 sts, skip next 2 dc, (dc, ch 2, dc) in next sc, skip next dc, sc in next 3 dc, skip next 2 sts, (dc, ch 2, dc) in last sc: {115-123}{131-139-147} sts and {28-30}{32-34-36} ch-2 sps.

Rows 50-62: Repeat Rows 46-49, 3 times; then repeat Row 46 once **more**: {169-181}{193-205-217} sts.

Row 63: Ch 1, turn; sc in first 3 dc, skip next 2 dc, (dc, ch 2, dc) in next sc, skip next dc, sc in next 3 dc, skip next 2 sts, (dc, ch 2, dc) in next sc, skip next 3 sts, sc in next 5 dc, ★ skip next 3 sts, dc in next sc, (ch 2, dc in same st) twice, skip next 3 sts, sc in next 5 dc; repeat from ★ across to last 16 sts, skip next 3 sts, (dc, ch 2, dc) in next sc, skip next 2 sts, sc in next 3 dc, skip next dc, (dc, ch 2, dc) in next sc, skip next 2 dc, sc in last 3 dc: {113-121}{129-137-145} sts and {26-28}{30-32-34} ch-2 sps.

Row 64: Ch 1, turn; sc in first 2 sc, † skip next 2 sts, 5 dc in next ch-2 sp, skip next 2 sts, sc in next sc, skip next 2 sts, 5 dc in next ch-2 sp †, skip next 2 sts, sc in next 3 sc, ★ skip next 2 sts, 4 dc in next ch-2 sp, dc in next dc, 4 dc in next ch-2 sp, skip next 2 sts, sc in next 3 sc; repeat from ★ across to last 11 sts, then repeat from † to † once, skip next 2 sts, sc in last 2 sc: {161-173}{185-197-209} sts.

Row 65: Ch 5, turn; dc in same st, † skip next 2 sts, sc in next 3 dc, skip next dc, (dc, ch 2, dc) in next sc, skip next dc, sc in next 3 dc †, skip next 2 sts, dc in next sc, (ch 2, dc in same st) twice, ★ skip next 3 sts, sc in next 5 dc, skip next 3 sts, dc in next sc, (ch 2, dc in same st) twice; repeat from ★ across to last 14 sts, then repeat from † to † once, skip next 2 sts, (dc, ch 2, dc) in last sc: {111-119}{127-135-143} sts and {28-30}{32-34-36} ch-2 sps.

Row 66: Ch 3, turn; 4 dc in next ch-2 sp, † skip next 2 sts, sc in next sc, skip next 2 sts, 5 dc in next ch-2 sp, skip next 2 sts, sc in next sc, skip next 2 sts, 4 dc in next ch-2 sp, dc in next dc †, 4 dc in next ch-2 sp, ★ skip next 2 sts, sc in next 3 sc, skip next 2 sts, 4 dc in next ch-2 sp, dc in next dc, 4 dc in next ch-2 sp; repeat from ★ across to last 11 sts, then repeat from † to † once: {165-177}{189-201-213} sts.

Row 67: Ch 1, turn; sc in first 3 dc, † skip next 2 dc, (dc, ch 2, dc) in next sc, skip next dc, sc in next 3 dc, skip next dc, (dc, ch 2, dc) in next sc †, skip next 2 dc, sc in next 5 dc, ★ skip next 3 sts, dc in next sc, (ch 2, dc in same st) twice, skip next 3 sts, sc in next 5 dc; repeat from ★ across to last 14 sts, then repeat from † to † once, skip next 2 dc, sc in last 3 dc: {113-121}{129-137-145} sts and {26-28}{30-32-34} ch-2 sps.

Rows 68-80: Repeat Rows 64-67, 3 times; then repeat Row 64 once **more**: {161-173}{185-197-209} sts.

Finish off.

ARMHOLE SHAPING

Row 1: With **right** side facing, skip first 32 sts and join Maroon with sc in next dc *(see Joining With Sc, page 58)*; sc in next 2 dc, skip next 3 sts, dc in next sc, (ch 2, dc in same st) twice, ★ skip next 3 sts, sc in next 5 dc, skip next 3 sts, dc in next sc, (ch 2, dc in same st) twice; repeat from ★ {6-7}{8-9-10} times **more**, skip next 3 sts, sc in next 3 dc, leave remaining 32 sts unworked: {65-73}{81-89-97} sts and {16-18}{20-22-24} ch-2 sps.

Row 2: Ch 1, turn; sc in first 2 sc, skip next 2 sts, 4 dc in next ch-2 sp, dc in next dc, 4 dc in next ch-2 sp, ★ skip next 2 sts, sc in next 3 sc, skip next 2 sts, 4 dc in next ch-2 sp, dc in next dc, 4 dc in next ch-2 sp; repeat from ★ across to last 4 sts, skip next 2 sts, sc in last 2 sc: {97-109}{121-133-145} sts.

Sizes Extra Large, 2X-Large, 3X-Large, and 4X-Large Only

Row 3 (Decrease row): Turn; slip st in first 6 sts, ch 1, sc in next 3 dc, skip next 3 sts, dc in next sc, (ch 2, dc in same st) twice, ★ skip next 3 sts, sc in next 5 dc, skip next 3 sts, dc in next sc, (ch 2, dc in same st) twice; repeat from ★ across to last 12 sts, skip next 3 sts, sc in next 3 dc, leave remaining 6 sts unworked: {65}{73-81-89} sts and {16}{18-20-22} ch-2 sps.

Instructions continued on page 48.

Row 4: Ch 1, turn; sc in first 2 sc, skip next 2 sts, 4 dc in next ch-2 sp, dc in next dc, 4 dc in next ch-2 sp, ★ skip next 2 sts, sc in next 3 sc, skip next 2 sts, 4 dc in next ch-2 sp, dc in next dc, 4 dc in next ch-2 sp; repeat from ★ across to last 4 sts, skip next 2 sts, sc in last 2 sc: {97}{109-121-133} sts.

Sizes 2X-Large, 3X-Large, and 4X-Large Only
Rows 5 thru {6-6-8}: Repeat Rows 3 and 4, {1-1-2} time(s): {97-109-109} sts.

All Sizes
Next Row: Ch 5, turn; dc in same st, skip next 3 sts, sc in next 5 dc, ★ skip next 3 sts, dc in next sc, (ch 2, dc in same st) twice, skip next 3 sts, sc in next 5 dc; repeat from ★ across to last 4 sts, skip next 3 sts, (dc, ch 2, dc) in last sc: {65-65}{65-73-73} sts and {16-16}{16-18-18} ch-2 sps.

Repeat Rows 2-5 of Body, {5-5}{5-6-6} times: {65-65}{65-73-73} sts and {16-16}{16-18-18} ch-2 sps.

LEFT SHOULDER SHAPING
Row 1: Ch 3, turn; 4 dc in next ch-2 sp, ★ skip next 2 sts, sc in next 3 sc, skip next 2 sts, 4 dc in next ch-2 sp, dc in next dc, 4 dc in next ch-2 sp; repeat from ★ once **more**, skip next 2 sts, sc in next 2 sc, leave remaining sts unworked: 31 sts.

Row 2: Turn; slip st in first 6 sts, ch 1, sc in next 3 dc, skip next 3 sts, dc in next sc, (ch 2, dc in same st) twice, skip next 3 sts, sc in next 5 dc, skip next 3 sts, dc in next sc, (ch 2, dc in same st) twice, skip next 3 sts, sc in last 3 dc: 17 sts and 4 ch-2 sps.

Row 3: Ch 1, turn; sc in first 2 sc, skip next 2 sts, 4 dc in next ch-2 sp, dc in next dc, 4 dc in next ch-2 sp, skip next 2 sts, sc in next 3 sc, skip next 2 sts, 4 dc in next ch-2 sp, dc in next dc, 4 dc in next ch-2 sp, skip next 2 sts, sc in last 2 sc: 25 sts.

Row 4: Ch 5, turn; dc in same st, skip next 3 sts, sc in next 5 dc, skip next 3 sts, dc in next sc, (ch 2, dc in same st) twice, skip next 3 sts, sc in next 5 dc, skip next 3 sts, (dc, ch 2, dc) in last sc: 17 sts and 4 ch-2 sps.

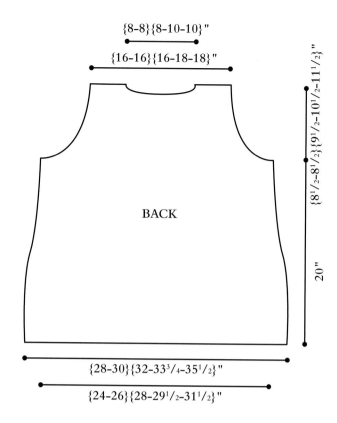

{8-8}{8-10-10}"
{16-16}{16-18-18}"
{8½-8½}{9½-10½-11½}"
20"
BACK
{28-30}{32-33¾-35½}"
{24-26}{28-29½-31½}"

Row 5: Ch 1, turn; skip first dc, 2 sc in next ch-2 sp, skip next 2 sts, sc in next 3 sc, skip next 2 sts, 4 dc in next ch-2 sp, dc in next dc, 4 dc in next ch-2 sp, skip next 2 sts, sc in next 3 sc, skip next 2 sts, 4 dc in next ch-2 sp, dc in last dc; finish off: 22 sts.

RIGHT SHOULDER SHAPING
Row 1: With **wrong** side facing, skip next {6-6}{6-8-8} ch-2 sps and next 2 sc from Left Shoulder and join Maroon with sc in next sc; sc in next sc, ★ skip next 2 sts, 4 dc in next ch-2 sp, dc in next dc, 4 dc in next ch-2 sp, skip next 2 sts, sc in next 3 sc; repeat from ★ once **more**, skip next 2 sts, 4 dc in next ch-2 sp, dc in last dc: 31 sts.

Row 2: Ch 1, turn; sc in first 3 dc, skip next 3 sts, dc in next sc, (ch 2, dc in same st) twice, skip next 3 sts, sc in next 5 dc, skip next 3 sts, dc in next sc, (ch 2, dc in same st) twice, skip next 3 sts, sc in next 3 dc, leave remaining 6 sts unworked: 17 sts and 4 ch-2 sps.

Row 3: Ch 1, turn; sc in first 2 sc, skip next 2 sts, 4 dc in next ch-2 sp, dc in next dc, 4 dc in next ch-2 sp, skip next 2 sts, sc in next 3 sc, skip next 2 sts, 4 dc in next ch-2 sp, dc in next dc, 4 dc in next ch-2 sp, skip next 2 sts, sc in last 2 sc: 25 sts.

Row 4: Ch 5, turn; dc in same st, skip next 3 sts, sc in next 5 dc, skip next 3 sts, dc in next sc, (ch 2, dc in same st) twice, skip next 3 sts, sc in next 5 dc, skip next 3 sts, (dc, ch 2, dc) in last sc: 17 sts and 4 ch-2 sps.

Row 5: Ch 3, turn; 4 dc in next ch-2 sp, skip next 2 sts, sc in next 3 sc, skip next 2 sts, 4 dc in next ch-2 sp, dc in next dc, 4 dc in next ch-2 sp, skip next 2 sts, sc in next 3 sc, skip next 2 sts, 2 sc in next ch-2 sp, leave last dc unworked; finish off: 22 sts.

Front

BODY

Rows 1-56: Work same as Back; at the end of Row 56, change to Rust in last sc made *(Fig. 4, page 59)*: {169-181}{193-205-217} sts.

Rows 57-70: Work same as Back; at the end of Row 70, change to Maroon in last dc made: {165-177}{189-201-213} sts.

Rows 71 and 72: Work same as Back: {161-173}{185-197-209} sts.

LEFT NECK SHAPING

Row 1: Ch 5, turn; dc in same st, skip next 2 sts, sc in next 3 dc, skip next dc, (dc, ch 2, dc) in next sc, skip next dc, sc in next 3 dc, skip next 2 sts, dc in next sc, (ch 2, dc in same st) twice, † skip next 3 sts, sc in next 5 dc, skip next 3 sts, dc in next sc, (ch 2, dc in same st) twice †; repeat from † to † once **more**, skip next 3 sts, sc in next 2 dc, working in Back Loops Only *(Fig. 2, page 58)*, sc in next 3 dc, place marker in free loop *(Fig. 3a, page 59)* of first dc worked into for Right Neck Shaping, skip next 3 sts, dc in next sc, (ch 2, dc in same st) twice, repeat from † to † {6-7}{8-9-10} times, skip next 3 sts, sc in next 3 dc, leave remaining sts unworked: {88-96}{104-112-120} sts and {22-24}{26-28-30} ch-2 sps.

Row 2 (Decrease row): Ch 1, turn; skip first sc, sc in next 2 sc, skip next dc, 4 dc in next ch-2 sp, dc in next dc, 4 dc in next ch-2 sp, ★ skip next 2 sts, sc in next 3 sc, skip next 2 sts, 4 dc in next ch-2 sp, dc in next dc, 4 dc in next ch-2 sp; repeat from ★ across to last 11 sts, skip next 2 sts, sc in next sc, skip next 2 sts, 5 dc in next ch-2 sp, skip next 2 sts, sc in next sc, skip next 2 sts, 4 dc in next ch-2 sp, dc in last dc: {131-143}{155-167-179} sts.

Row 3 (Decrease row): Ch 1, turn; sc in first 3 dc, skip next 2 dc, (dc, ch 2, dc) in next sc, skip next dc, sc in next 3 dc, skip next dc, (dc, ch 2, dc) in next sc, skip next 2 dc, sc in next 5 dc, skip next 3 sts, dc in next sc, (ch 2, dc in same st) twice, ★ skip next 3 sts, sc in next 5 dc, skip next 3 sts, dc in next sc, (ch 2, dc in same st) twice; repeat from ★ across to last 12 sts, skip next 3 sts, sc in next 4 dc, leave remaining 5 sts unworked: {86-94}{102-110-118} sts and {20-22}{24-26-28} ch-2 sps.

Instructions continued on page 50.

Row 4 (Decrease row): Ch 1, turn; skip first sc, sc in next 3 sc, skip next dc, 4 dc in next ch-2 sp, dc in next dc, 4 dc in next ch-2 sp, skip next 2 sts, sc in next 3 sc, ★ skip next 2 sts, 4 dc in next ch-2 sp, dc in next dc, 4 dc in next ch-2 sp, skip next 2 sts, sc in next 3 sc; repeat from ★ across to last 11 sts, skip next 2 sts, 5 dc in next ch-2 sp, skip next 2 sts, sc in next sc, skip next 2 sts, 5 dc in next ch-2 sp, skip next 2 sts, sc in last 2 sc: {124-136}{148-160-172} sts.

Row 5 (Decrease row): Ch 5, turn; dc in same st, skip next 2 sts, sc in next 3 dc, skip next dc, (dc, ch 2, dc) in next sc, skip next dc, sc in next 3 dc, skip next 2 sts, dc in next sc, (ch 2, dc in same st) twice, ★ skip next 3 sts, sc in next 5 dc, skip next 3 sts, dc in next sc, (ch 2, dc in same st) twice; repeat from ★ across to last 13 sts, skip next 3 sts, sc in next 3 dc, leave remaining 7 sts unworked: {80-88}{96-104-112} sts and {20-22}{24-26-28} ch-2 sps.

Rows 6-8: Repeat Rows 2-4: {112-124}{136-148-160} sts.

Finish off.

ARMHOLE SHAPING

Row 1: With **right** side facing, skip first 32 sts and join Maroon with sc in next dc; sc in next 2 dc, skip next 3 sts, dc in next sc, (ch 2, dc in same st) twice, ★ skip next 3 sts, sc in next 5 dc, skip next 3 sts, dc in next sc, (ch 2, dc in same st) twice; repeat from ★ across to last 13 sts, skip next 3 sts, sc in next 3 dc, leave remaining 7 sts unworked: {49-57}{65-73-81} sts and {12-14}{16-18-20} ch-2 sps.

Row 2 (Decrease row): Ch 1, turn; skip first sc, sc in next 2 sc, skip next dc, 4 dc in next ch-2 sp, dc in next dc, 4 dc in next ch-2 sp, ★ skip next 2 sts, sc in next 3 sc, skip next 2 sts, 4 dc in next ch-2 sp, dc in next dc, 4 dc in next ch-2 sp; repeat from ★ across to last 4 sts, skip next 2 sts, sc in last 2 sc: {73-85}{97-109-121} sts.

Size Large Only

Row 3: Ch 5, turn; dc in same st, ★ skip next 3 sts, sc in next 5 dc, skip next 3 sts, dc in next sc, (ch 2, dc in same st) twice; repeat from ★ across to last 12 sts, skip next 3 sts, sc in next 4 dc, leave remaining 5 sts unworked: 46 sts and 11 ch-2 sps.

Row 4 (Decrease row): Ch 1, turn; skip first sc, sc in next 3 sc, skip next dc, 4 dc in next ch-2 sp, dc in next dc, 4 dc in next ch-2 sp, skip next 2 sts, sc in next 3 sc, ★ skip next 2 sts, 4 dc in next ch-2 sp, dc in next dc, 4 dc in next ch-2 sp, skip next 2 sts, sc in next 3 sc; repeat from ★ across to last 3 sts, skip next 2 sts, 4 dc in next ch-2 sp, dc in last dc: 68 sts.

Row 5 (Decrease row): Ch 1, turn; sc in first 3 dc, skip next 3 sts, dc in next sc, (ch 2, dc in same st) twice, ★ skip next 3 sts, sc in next 5 dc, skip next 3 sts, dc in next sc, (ch 2, dc in same st) twice; repeat from ★ across to last 13 sts, skip next 3 sts, sc in next 4 dc, leave remaining 6 sts unworked: 42 sts and 10 ch-2 sps.

Row 6 (Decrease row): Ch 1, turn; skip first sc, sc in next 3 sc, skip next dc, 4 dc in next ch-2 sp, dc in next dc, 4 dc in next ch-2 sp, ★ skip next 2 sts, sc in next 3 sc, skip next 2 sts, 4 dc in next ch-2 sp, dc in next dc, 4 dc in next ch-2 sp; repeat from ★ across to last 4 sts, skip next 2 sts, sc in last 2 sc: 62 sts.

Row 7 (Decrease row): Ch 5, turn; dc in same st, ★ skip next 3 sts, sc in next 5 dc, skip next 3 sts, dc in next sc, (ch 2, dc in same st) twice; repeat from ★ across to last 13 sts, skip next 3 sts, sc in next 4 dc, leave remaining 6 sts unworked: 38 sts and 9 ch-2 sps.

Rows 8-15: Repeat Rows 4-7 twice: 22 sts and 5 ch-2 sps.

Sizes Extra Large, 2X-Large, 3X-Large, and 4X-Large Only

Row 3 (Decrease row): Turn; slip st in first 6 sts, ch 1, sc in next 3 dc, skip next 3 sts, dc in next sc, (ch 2, dc in same st) twice, ★ skip next 3 sts, sc in next 5 dc, skip next 3 sts, dc in next sc, (ch 2, dc in same st) twice; repeat from ★ across to last 12 sts, skip next 3 sts, sc in next 4 dc, leave remaining 5 sts unworked: {50}{58-66-74} sts and {12}{14-16-18} ch-2 sps.

Row 4 (Decrease row): Ch 1, turn; skip first sc, sc in next 3 sc, skip next dc, 4 dc in next ch-2 sp, dc in next dc, 4 dc in next ch-2 sp, ★ skip next 2 sts, sc in next 3 sc, skip next 2 sts, 4 dc in next ch-2 sp, dc in next dc, 4 dc in next ch-2 sp; repeat from ★ across to last 4 sts, skip next 2 sts, sc in last 2 sc: {74}{86-98-110} sts.

Sizes 2X-Large, 3X-Large and 4X-Large Only
Row 5 (Decrease row)**:** Turn; slip st in first 6 sts, ch 1, sc in next 3 dc, skip next 3 sts, dc in next sc, (ch 2, dc in same st) twice, ★ skip next 3 sts, sc in next 5 dc, skip next 3 sts, dc in next sc, (ch 2, dc in same st) twice; repeat from ★ across to last 13 sts, skip next 3 sts, sc in next 4 dc, leave remaining 6 sts unworked: {50-58-66} sts and {12-14-16} ch-2 sps.

Row 6: Repeat Row 4: {74-86-98} sts.

Size 4X-Large Only
Rows 7 and 8: Repeat Rows 5 and 6: 86 sts.

Sizes Extra Large, 2X-Large, 3X-Large, and 4X-Large Only
Next Row: Ch 5, turn; dc in same st, ★ skip next 3 sts, sc in next 5 dc, skip next 3 sts, dc in next sc, (ch 2, dc in same st) twice; repeat from ★ across to last 13 sts, skip next 3 sts, sc in next 4 dc, leave remaining 6 sts unworked: {46}{46-54-54} sts and {11}{11-13-13} ch-2 sps.

Next Decrease Row: Ch 1, turn; skip first sc, sc in next 3 sc, skip next dc, 4 dc in next ch-2 sp, dc in next dc, 4 dc in next ch-2 sp, skip next 2 sts, sc in next 3 sc, ★ skip next 2 sts, 4 dc in next ch-2 sp, dc in next dc, 4 dc in next ch-2 sp, skip next 2 sts, sc in next 3 sc; repeat from ★ across to last 3 sts, skip next 2 sts, 4 dc in next ch-2 sp, dc in last dc: {68}{68-80-80} sts.

Next Decrease Row: Ch 1, turn; sc in first 3 dc, skip next 3 sts, dc in next sc, (ch 2, dc in same st) twice, ★ skip next 3 sts, sc in next 5 dc, skip next 3 sts, dc in next sc, (ch 2, dc in same st) twice; repeat from ★ across to last 13 sts, skip next 3 sts, sc in next 4 dc, leave remaining 6 sts unworked: {42}{42-50-50} sts and {10}{10-12-12} ch-2 sps.

Next Decrease Row: Ch 1, turn; skip first sc, sc in next 3 sc, skip next dc, 4 dc in next ch-2 sp, dc in next dc, 4 dc in next ch-2 sp, ★ skip next 2 sts, sc in next 3 sc, skip next 2 sts, 4 dc in next ch-2 sp, dc in next dc, 4 dc in next ch-2 sp; repeat from ★ across to last 4 sts, skip next 2 sts, sc in last 2 sc: {62}{62-74-74} sts.

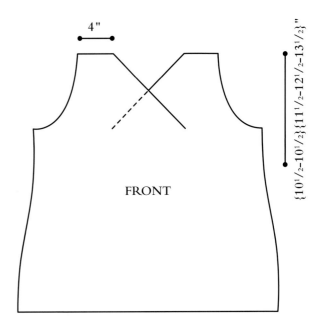

4"

{10½-10½}{11½-12½-13½}"

FRONT

Next Decrease Row: Ch 5, turn; dc in same st, ★ skip next 3 sts, sc in next 5 dc, skip next 3 sts, dc in next sc, (ch 2, dc in same st) twice; repeat from ★ across to last 13 sts, skip next 3 sts, sc in next 4 dc, leave remaining 6 sts unworked: {38}{38-46-46} sts and {9}{9-11-11} ch-2 sps.

Repeat last 4 rows, {2}{2-3-3} times: 22 sts and 5 ch-2 sps.

All Sizes
Row 1: Ch 1, turn; skip first sc, sc in next 2 sc, ★ skip next 2 sts, 4 dc in next ch-2 sp, dc in next dc, 4 dc in next ch-2 sp, skip next 2 sts, sc in next 3 sc; repeat from ★ once **more**, skip next 2 sts, 4 dc in next ch-2 sp, dc in last dc: 31 sts.

Row 2: Ch 1, turn; sc in first 3 dc, ★ skip next 3 sts, dc in next sc, (ch 2, dc in same st) twice, skip next 3 sts, sc in next 5 dc; repeat from ★ once **more**, skip next 3 sts, (dc, ch 2, dc) in last sc: 21 sts and 5 ch-2 sps.

Row 3: Ch 3, turn; 4 dc in next ch-2 sp, ★ skip next 2 sts, sc in next 3 dc, skip next 2 sts, 4 dc in next ch-2 sp, dc in next dc, 4 dc in next ch-2 sp; repeat from ★ once **more**, skip next 2 sts, sc in last 2 sc: 31 sts.

Instructions continued on page 52.

Row 4: Ch 5, turn; dc in same st, ★ skip next 3 sts, sc in next 5 dc, skip next 3 sts, dc in next sc, (ch 2, dc in same st) twice; repeat from ★ across to last 6 sts, skip next 3 sts, sc in last 3 dc: 21 sts and 5 ch-2 sps.

Row 5: Ch 1, turn; sc in first 2 sc, ★ skip next 2 sts, 4 dc in next ch-2 sp, dc in next dc, 4 dc in next ch-2 sp, skip next 2 sts, sc in next 3 sc; repeat from ★ across last 3 sts, skip next 2 sts, 4 dc in next ch-2 sp, dc in last dc: 31 sts.

Repeat Rows 2-5 for pattern until Left Front measures same as Back to Shoulder Shaping, ending by working Row 3.

SHOULDER SHAPING

Row 1: Turn; slip st in first 6 sts, ch 1, sc in next 3 dc, skip next 3 sts, dc in next sc, (ch 2, dc in same st) twice, skip next 3 sts, sc in next 5 dc, skip next 3 sts, dc in next sc, (ch 2, dc in same st) twice, skip next 3 sts, sc in last 3 dc: 17 sts and 4 ch-2 sps.

Row 2: Ch 1, turn; sc in first 2 sc, skip next 2 sts, 4 dc in next ch-2 sp, dc in next dc, 4 dc in next ch-2 sp, skip next 2 sts, sc in next 3 sc, skip next 2 sts, 4 dc in next ch-2 sp, dc in next dc, 4 dc in next ch-2 sp, skip next 2 sts, sc in last 2 sc: 25 sts.

Row 3: Ch 5, dc in same st, skip next 3 sts, sc in next 5 dc, skip next 3 sts, dc in next sc, (ch 2, dc in same st) twice, skip next 3 sts, sc in next 5 dc, skip next 3 sts, (dc, ch 2, dc) in last sc: 17 sts and 4 ch-2 sps.

Row 4: Ch 1, turn; skip first dc, 2 sc in next ch-2 sp, skip next 2 sts, sc in next 3 sc, skip next 2 sts, 4 dc in next ch-2 sp, dc in next dc, 4 dc in next ch-2 sp, skip next 2 sts, sc in next 3 sc, skip next 2 sts, 4 dc in next ch-2 sp, dc in last dc; finish off: 22 sts.

RIGHT NECK SHAPING

Row 1: With **right** side facing, working **behind** sts on Left Front Neck in free loops of sts **and** in unworked sts on Row 72, join Maroon with sc in marked dc; sc in next 2 dc, skip next 3 sts, dc in next sc, (ch 2, dc in same st) twice, ★ skip next 3 sts, sc in next 5 dc, skip next 3 sts, dc in next sc, (ch 2, dc in same st) twice; repeat from ★ across to last 14 sts, skip next 2 sts, sc in next 3 dc, skip next dc, (dc, ch 2, dc) in next sc, skip next dc, sc in next 3 dc, skip next 2 sts, (dc, ch 2, dc) in last sc: {88-96}{104-112-120} sts and {22-24}{26-30-32} ch-2 sps.

Row 2 (Decrease row)**:** Ch 3, turn; 4 dc in next ch-2 sp, skip next 2 sts, sc in next sc, skip next 2 sts, 5 dc in next ch-2 sp, skip next 2 sts, sc in next sc, skip next 2 sts, 4 dc in next ch-2 sp, dc in next dc, 4 dc in next ch-2 sp, ★ skip next 2 sts, sc in next 3 sc, skip next 2 sts, 4 dc in next ch-2 sp, dc in next dc, 4 dc in next ch-2 sp; repeat from ★ across to last 4 sts, skip next dc, sc in next 2 sc, leave last sc unworked: {131-143}{155-167-179} sts.

Row 3 (Decrease row)**:** Turn; slip st in first 5 sts, ch 1, sc in next 4 dc, ★ skip next 3 sts, dc in next sc, (ch 2, dc in same st) twice, skip next 3 sts, sc in next 5 dc; repeat from ★ across to last 14 sts, skip next 2 dc, (dc, ch 2, dc) in next sc, skip next dc, sc in next 3 dc, skip next dc, (dc, ch 2, dc) in next sc, skip next 2 dc, sc in last 3 dc: {86-94}{102-110-118} sts and {20-22}{24-26-28} ch-2 sps.

Row 4 (Decrease row)**:** Ch 1, turn; sc in first 2 sc, skip next 2 sts, 5 dc in next ch-2 sp, skip next 2 sts, sc in next sc, skip next 2 sts, 5 dc in next ch-2 sp, skip next 2 sts, sc in next 3 sc, ★ skip next 2 sts, 4 dc in next ch-2 sp, dc in next dc, 4 dc in next ch-2 sp, skip next 2 sts, sc in next 3 sc; repeat from ★ across, leave last sc unworked: {124-136}{148-160-172} sts.

Row 5 (Decrease row): Turn; slip st in first 7 sts, ch 1, sc in next 3 dc, skip next 3 sts, dc in next sc, (ch 2, dc in same st) twice, ★ skip next 3 sts, sc in next 5 dc, skip next 3 sts, dc in next sc, (ch 2, dc in same st) twice; repeat from ★ across to last 14 sts, skip next 2 sts, sc in next 3 dc, skip next dc, (dc, ch 2, dc) in next sc, skip next dc, sc in next 3 dc, skip next 2 sts, (dc, ch 2, dc) in last sc: {80-88}{96-104-112} sts and {20-22}{24-26-28} ch-2 sps

Rows 6-8: Repeat Rows 2-4: {112-124}{136-148-160} sts.

Do **not** finish off.

ARMHOLE SHAPING

Row 1: Turn; slip st in first 7 sts, ch 1, sc in next 3 dc, skip next 3 sts, dc in next sc, (ch 2, dc in same st) twice, ★ skip next 3 sts, sc in next 5 dc, skip next 3 sts, dc in next sc, (ch 2, dc in same st) twice; repeat from ★ across to last 38 sts, skip next 3 sts, sc in next 3 dc, leave remaining sts unworked: {49-57}{65-73-81} sts and {12-14}{16-18-20} ch-2 sps.

Row 2 (Decrease row): Ch 1, turn; sc in first 2 sc, skip next 2 sts, 4 dc in next ch-2 sp, dc in next dc, 4 dc in next ch-2 sp, ★ skip next 2 sts, sc in next 3 sc, skip next 2 sts, 4 dc in next ch-2 sp, dc in next dc, 4 dc in next ch-2 sp; repeat from ★ across to last 4 sts, skip next dc, sc in next 2 sc, leave last sc unworked: {73-85}{97-109-121} sts.

Size Large Only

Row 3: Turn; slip st in first 5 sts, ch 1, sc in next 4 dc, ★ skip next 3 sts, dc in next sc, (ch 2, dc in same st) twice, skip next 3 sts, sc in next 5 dc; repeat from ★ across to last 4 sts, skip next 3 sts, (dc, ch 2, dc) in last sc: 46 sts and 11 ch-2 sps.

Row 4 (Decrease row): Ch 3, turn; 4 dc in next ch-2 sp, skip next 2 sts, sc in next 3 sc, ★ skip next 2 sts, 4 dc in next ch-2 sp, dc in next dc, 4 dc in next ch-2 sp, skip next 2 sts, sc in next 3 sc; repeat from ★ across, leave last sc unworked: 68 sts.

Row 5 (Decrease row): Turn; slip st in first 6 sts, ch 1, sc in next 4 dc, skip next 3 sts, dc in next sc, (ch 2, dc in same st) twice, ★ skip next 3 sts, sc in next 5 dc, skip next 3 sts, dc in next sc, (ch 2, dc in same st) twice; repeat from ★ across to last 6 sts, skip next 3 sts, sc in last 3 dc: 42 sts and 10 ch-2 sps.

Instructions continued on page 54.

Row 6 (Decrease row): Ch 1, turn; sc in first 2 sc, ★ skip next 2 sts, 4 dc in next ch-2 sp, dc in next dc, 4 dc in next ch-2 sp, skip next 2 sts, sc in next 3 sc; repeat from ★ across to last sc, leave last sc unworked: 62 sts.

Row 7 (Decrease row): Turn; slip st in first 6 sts, ch 1, sc in next 4 dc, ★ skip next 3 sts, dc in next sc, (ch 2, dc in same st) twice, skip next 3 sts, sc in next 5 dc; repeat from ★ across to last 4 sts, skip next 3 sts, (dc, ch 2, dc) in last sc: 38 sts and 9 ch-2 sps.

Rows 8-15: Repeat Rows 4-7 twice: 22 sts and 5 ch-2 sps.

Sizes Extra Large, 2X-Large, 3X-Large, and 4X-Large Only
Row 3 (Decrease row): Turn; slip st in first 5 sts, ch 1, sc in next 4 dc, skip next 3 sts, dc in next sc, (ch 2, dc in same st) twice, ★ skip next 3 sts, sc in next 5 dc, skip next 3 sts, dc in next sc, (ch 2, dc in same st) twice; repeat from ★ across to last 12 sts, skip next 3 sts, sc in next 3 dc, leave remaining sts unworked: {50}{58-66-74} sts and {12}{14-16-18} ch-2 sps.

Row 4 (Decrease row): Ch 1, turn; sc in first 2 sc, ★ skip next 2 sts, 4 dc in next ch-2 sp, dc in next dc, 4 dc in next ch-2 sp, skip next 2 sts, sc in next 3 sc; repeat from ★ across to last sc, leave last sc unworked: {74}{86-98-110} sts.

Sizes 2X-Large, 3X-Large and 4X-Large Only
Row 5 (Decrease row): Turn; slip st in first 6 sts, ch 1, sc in next 4 dc, skip next 3 sts, dc in next sc, (ch 2, dc in same st) twice, ★ skip next 3 sts, sc in next 5 dc, skip next 3 sts, dc in next sc, (ch 2, dc in same st) twice; repeat from ★ across to last 12 sts, skip next 3 sts, sc in next 3 dc, leave remaining 6 sts unworked: {50-58-66} sts and {12-14-16} ch-2 sps.

Row 6: Repeat Row 4: {74-86-98} sts.

Size 4X-Large Only
Rows 7 and 8: Repeat Rows 5 and 6: 86 sts.

Sizes Extra Large, 2X-Large, 3X-Large, and 4X-Large Only
Next Row: Ch 5, turn; dc in same st, ★ skip next 3 sts, sc in next 5 dc, skip next 3 sts, dc in next sc, (ch 2, dc in same st) twice; repeat from ★ across to last 13 sts, skip next 3 sts, sc in next 4 dc, leave remaining 6 sts unworked: {46}{46-54-54} sts and {11}{11-13-13} ch-2 sps.

Next Decrease Row: Ch 1, turn; skip first sc, sc in next 3 sc, skip next dc, 4 dc in next ch-2 sp, dc in next dc, 4 dc in next ch-2 sp, skip next 2 sts, sc in next 3 sc, ★ skip next 2 sts, 4 dc in next ch-2 sp, dc in next dc, 4 dc in next ch-2 sp, skip next 2 sts, sc in next 3 sc; repeat from ★ across to last 3 sts, skip next 2 sts, 4 dc in next ch-2 sp, dc in last dc: {68}{68-80-80} sts.

Next Decrease Row: Ch 1, turn; sc in first 3 dc, skip next 3 sts, dc in next sc, (ch 2, dc in same st) twice, ★ skip next 3 sts, sc in next 5 dc, skip next 3 sts, dc in next sc, (ch 2, dc in same st) twice; repeat from ★ across to last 13 sts, skip next 3 sts, sc in next 4 dc, leave remaining 6 sts unworked: {42}{42-50-50} sts and {10}{10-12-12} ch-2 sps.

Next Decrease Row: Ch 1, turn; skip first sc, sc in next 3 sc, skip next dc, 4 dc in next ch-2 sp, dc in next dc, 4 dc in next ch-2 sp, ★ skip next 2 sts, sc in next 3 sc, skip next 2 sts, 4 dc in next ch-2 sp, dc in next dc, 4 dc in next ch-2 sp; repeat from ★ across to last 4 sts, skip next 2 sts, sc in last 2 sc: {62}{62-72-72} sts.

Next Decrease Row: Ch 5, turn; dc in same st, ★ skip next 3 sts, sc in next 5 dc, skip next 3 sts, dc in next sc, (ch 2, dc in same st) twice; repeat from ★ across to last 13 sts, skip next 3 sts, sc in next 4 dc, leave remaining 6 sts unworked: {38}{38-46-46} sts and {9}{9-11-11} ch-2 sps.

Repeat last 4 rows, {2}{2-3-3} times: 22 sts and 5 ch-2 sps.

ALL SIZES

Row 1: Ch 1, turn; skip first sc, sc in next 2 sc, ★ skip next 2 sts, 4 dc in next ch-2 sp, dc in next dc, 4 dc in next ch-2 sp, skip next 2 sts, sc in next 3 sc; repeat from ★ across to last 3 sts, skip next 2 sts, 4 dc in next ch-2 sp, dc in last dc: 31 sts.

Row 2: Ch 1, turn; sc in first 3 dc, ★ skip next 3 sts, dc in next sc, (ch 2, dc in same st) twice, skip next 3 sts, sc in next 5 dc; repeat from ★ across to last 4 sts, skip next 3 sts, (dc, ch 2, dc) in last sc: 21 sts and 5 ch-2 sps.

Row 3: Ch 3, turn; 4 dc in next ch-2 sp, ★ skip next 2 sts, sc in next 3 dc, skip next 2 sts, 4 dc in next ch-2 sp, dc in next dc, 4 dc in next ch-2 sp; repeat from ★ across to last 4 sts, skip next 2 sts, sc in last 2 sc: 31 sts.

Row 4: Ch 5, turn; dc in same st, ★ skip next 3 sts, sc in next 5 dc, skip next 3 sts, dc in next sc, (ch 2, dc in same st) twice; repeat from ★ across to last 6 sts, skip next 3 sts, sc in last 3 dc: 21 sts and 5 ch-2 sps.

Row 5: Ch 1, turn; sc in first 2 sc, ★ skip next 2 sts, 4 dc in next ch-2 sp, dc in next dc, 4 dc in next ch-2 sp, skip next 2 sts, sc in next 3 sc; repeat from ★ across last 3 sts, skip next 2 sts, 4 dc in next ch-2 sp, dc in last dc: 31 sts.

Repeat Rows 2-5 for pattern until Right Front measures same as Back to Shoulder Shaping, ending by working Row 3.

SHOULDER SHAPING

Row 1: Ch 1, turn; sc in first 3 dc, skip next 3 sts, dc in next sc, (ch 2, dc in same st) twice, skip next 3 sts, sc in next 5 dc, skip next 3 sts, dc in next sc, (ch 2, dc in same st) twice, skip next 3 sts, sc in next 3 dc, leave remaining 6 sts unworked: 17 sts and 4 ch-2 sps.

Row 2: Ch 1, turn; sc in first 2 sc, skip next 2 sts, 4 dc in next ch-2 sp, dc in next dc, 4 dc in next ch-2 sp, skip next 2 sts, sc in next 3 sc, skip next 2 sts, 4 dc in next ch-2 sp, dc in next dc, 4 dc in next ch-2 sp, skip next 2 sts, sc in last 2 sc: 25 sts.

Row 3: Ch 5, turn; dc in same st, skip next 3 sts, sc in next 5 dc, skip next 3 sts, dc in next sc, (ch 2, dc in same st) twice, skip next 3 sts, sc in next 5 dc, skip next 3 sts, (dc, ch 2, dc) in last sc: 17 sts and 4 ch-2 sps.

Row 4: Ch 3, turn; 4 dc in next ch-2 sp, skip next 2 sts, sc in next 3 sc, skip next 2 sts, 4 dc in next ch-2 sp, dc in next dc, 4 dc in next ch-2 sp, skip next 2 sts, sc in next 3 sc, skip next 2 sts, 2 sc in next ch-2 sp, leave last dc unworked; finish off: 22 sts.

Sleeve (Make 2)

BODY

With Maroon, ch {162-174}{186-198-210}.

Rows 1-8: Work same as Back: {157-169}{181-193-205} sts.

Finish off.

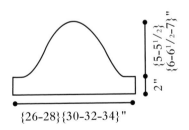

{5-5½}
{6-6½-7}"

2"

{26-28}{30-32-34}"

Instructions continued on page 56.

CAP SHAPING

Row 1: With **right** side facing, skip first 16 sts and join Maroon with sc in next dc; sc in next 4 dc, ★ skip next 3 sts, dc in next sc, (ch 2, dc in same st) twice, skip next 3 sts, sc in next 5 dc; repeat from ★ across to last 16 sts, leave remaining sts unworked: {85-93} {101-109-117} sts and {20-22}{24-26-28} ch-2 sps.

Row 2 (Decrease row): Ch 1, turn; skip first sc, sc in next 3 sc, ★ skip next 2 sts, 4 dc in next ch-2 sp, dc in next dc, 4 dc in next ch-2 sp, skip next 2 sts, sc in next 3 sc; repeat from ★ across to last sc, leave last sc unworked: {123-135}{147-159-171} sts.

Row 3 (Decrease row): Turn; slip st in first 5 sts, ch 1, sc in next 5 dc, ★ skip next 3 sts, dc in next sc, (ch 2, dc in same st) twice, skip next 3 sts, sc in next 5 dc; repeat from ★ across to last 5 sts, leave remaining sts unworked: {77-85}{93-101-109} sts and {18-20} {22-24-26} ch-2 sps.

Rows 4 thru {19-21}{23-25-27}: Repeat Rows 2 and 3, {8-9}{10-11-12} times: 13 sts and 2 ch-2 sps.

Last Row: Ch 1, turn; skip first sc, sc in next 3 sc, skip next 2 sts, 4 dc in next ch-2 sp, dc in next dc, 4 dc in next ch-2 sp, skip next 2 sts, sc in next 3 sc, leave last sc unworked; finish off: 15 sts.

Finishing

Sew shoulder seams. Sew Sleeves in place. Sew side and Sleeve seams.

Trim

Row 1: With **right** side facing, join Rust with sc in first sc on Right Front Neck; sc evenly across to last st on Left Front Neck.

Rows 2 and 3: Ch 1, turn; sc in each sc across, decreasing as necessary to keep Trim flat.

Finish off.

Tie (Make 2)

With Rust, ch {186-198}{210-222-234}.

Rows 1-14: Work same as Back.

Finish off.

With Rust, sew one Tie to each side seam at end of Rows 57-70 on Front.

General Instructions

Abbreviations

ch(s)	chain(s)
cm	centimeters
dc	double crochet(s)
hdc	half double crochet(s)
mm	millimeters
Rnd(s)	Round(s)
sc	single crochet(s)
sp(s)	space(s)
st(s)	stitch(es)
tr	treble crochet(s)
YO	yarn over

★ — work instructions following ★ as many **more** times as indicated in addition to the first time.

† to † or ♥ to ♥ — work all instructions from first † or ♥ to second † or ♥ **as many** times as specified.

( ) or [ ] — work enclosed instructions **as many** times as specified by the number immediately following **or** work all enclosed instructions in the stitch or space indicated **or** contains explanatory remarks.

colon (:) — the number(s) given after a colon at the end of a row or round denote(s) the number of stitches or spaces you should have on that row or round.

work even — work without increasing or decreasing in the established pattern.

Yarn Weight Symbol & Names	SUPER FINE 1	FINE 2	LIGHT 3	MEDIUM 4	BULKY 5	SUPER BULKY 6
Type of Yarns in Category	Sock, Fingering Baby	Sport, Baby	DK, Light Worsted	Worsted, Afghan, Aran	Chunky, Craft, Rug	Bulky, Roving
Crochet Gauge Ranges in Single Crochet to 4" (10 cm)	21-32 sts	16-20 sts	12-17 sts	11-14 sts	8-11 sts	5-9 sts
Advised Hook Size Range	B-1 to E-4	E-4 to 7	7 to I-9	I-9 to K-10.5	K-10.5 to M-13	M-13 and larger

CROCHET TERMINOLOGY	
UNITED STATES	**INTERNATIONAL**
slip stitch (slip st) =	single crochet (sc)
single crochet (sc) =	double crochet (dc)
half double crochet (hdc) =	half treble crochet (htr)
double crochet (dc) =	treble crochet (tr)
treble crochet (tr) =	double treble crochet (dtr)
double treble crochet (dtr) =	triple treble crochet (ttr)
triple treble crochet (tr tr) =	quadruple treble crochet (qtr)
skip =	miss

■□□□ BEGINNER	Projects for first-time crocheters using basic stitches. Minimal shaping.
■■□□ EASY	Projects using yarn with basic stitches, repetitive stitch patterns, simple color changes, and simple shaping and finishing.
■■■□ INTERMEDIATE	Projects using a variety of techniques, such as basic lace patterns or color patterns, mid-level shaping and finishing.
■■■■ EXPERIENCED	Projects with intricate stitch patterns, techniques and dimension, such as non-repeating patterns, multi-color techniques, fine threads, small hooks, detailed shaping and refined finishing.

CROCHET HOOKS												
U.S.	B-1	C-2	D-3	E-4	F-5	G-6	H-8	I-9	J-10	K-10½	N	P	Q
Metric - mm	2.25	2.75	3.25	3.5	3.75	4	5	5.5	6	6.5	9	10	15

Gauge

Exact gauge is essential for proper size. Before beginning your project, make the sample swatch given in the individual instructions in the yarn and hook specified. After completing the swatch, measure it, counting your stitches and rows/rounds carefully. If your swatch is larger or smaller than specified, **make another, changing hook size to get the correct gauge.** Keep trying until you find the size hook that will give you the specified gauge. Once proper gauge is obtained, measure width of garment approximately every 3" (7.5 cm) to be sure gauge remains consistent.

Joining with SC

When instructed to join with sc, begin with a slip knot on hook. Insert hook in stitch or space indicated, YO and pull up a loop, YO and draw through both loops on hook.

Joining with DC

When instructed to join with dc, begin with a slip knot on hook. YO, holding loop on hook, insert hook in stitch or space indicated, YO and pull up a loop (3 loops on hook), (YO and draw through 2 loops on hook) twice.

Zeros

To consolidate the length of an involved pattern, zeros are sometimes used so that all sizes can be combined. For example, increase every sixth row 5{1-0} time(s) means the first size would increase 5 times, the second size would increase once, and the largest size would do nothing.

Back Ridge

Work only in loops indicated by arrows *(Fig. 1)*.

Fig. 1

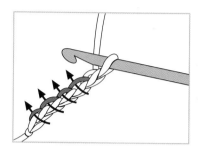

Back or Front Loop Only

Work only in loop(s) indicated by arrow *(Fig. 2)*.

Fig. 2

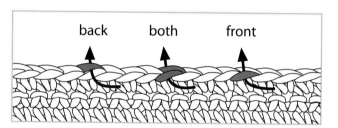

Free Loops

After working in Back or Front Loops Only on a row or round, there will be a ridge of unused loops. These are called the free loops. Later, when instructed to work in the free loops of the same row or round, work in these loops *(Fig. 3a)*.

When instructed to work in free loops of a chain, work in loop indicated by arrow *(Fig. 3b)*.

Fig. 3a

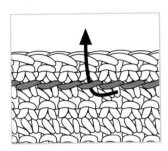

Fig. 3b

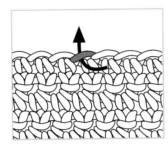

Changing Colors

Work the last stitch to within one step of completion, hook new yarn *(Fig. 4)* and draw through all loops on hook. Do **not** cut old yarn until instructed.

Fig. 4

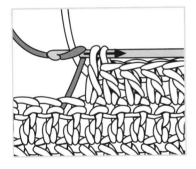

Working in Space Before a Stitch

When instructed to work in space **before** a stitch or in spaces **between** stitches, insert hook in space indicated by arrow *(Fig. 5)*.

Fig. 5

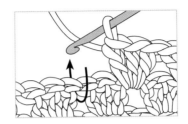

Twisted Cord

Cut 2 pieces of yarn, each 3 times as long as the desired finished length. Holding both pieces together, fasten one end to a stationary object **or** have another person hold it; twist until tight. Fold in half and let it twist upon itself, knot both ends and cut the loops on the folded end.

Yarn Information

The items in this leaflet were made using a variety of yarns. Any brand of the specified weight of yarn may be used. It is best to refer to the yardage/meters when determining how many balls or skeins to purchase. Remember, to achieve the same look, it is the weight of yarn that is important, not the brand of yarn. For your convenience, listed below are the specific yarns used to create our photography models.

COWL NECK TUNIC
Naturally Caron® Spa
#0008 Misty Taupe

PEASANT TOP
Red Heart® LusterSheen®
#0805 Natural

STOLE
Patons® Silk Bamboo
#85236 Moss

MOTIF BOLERO
Omega Sinfonia
#08 Black

FELTED HANDBAG
Cascade Yarns 220 Heathers
Blue - #4009
Cascade Yarns 220 Wool
Turquoise - #8891
Purple - #8888

A-LINE VEST
Lion Brand® Cotton-Ease®
Brown - #122 Taupe
Rose - #112 Berry

RIBBED WAIST TUNIC
Red Heart® Bamboo Wool
#3920 Cayenne

TIE BACK TUNIC
Berrocco® Ultra® Alpaca Fine
Maroon - #1282 Boysenberry Mix
Rust - #6280 Mahogany Mix

Production Team

Instructional Editor: Sarah J. Green
Technical Editor: Lois J. Long
Editorial Writer: Susan McManus Johnson
Senior Graphic Artist: Lora Puls
Graphic Artist: Becca Snider
Photo Stylist: Cora Holdaway
Photographer: Jason Masters